Sifting Through Science

Teacher's Guide

K–2
(can be adapted for Prekindergarten)

Skills
Exploring, Observing, Counting, Comparing, Describing,
Communicating, Predicting, Testing,
Visualizing and Graphing Data,
Sorting and Classifying, Applying

Concepts
Properties and Attributes, Repeatability of Results,
Substances, Floating and Sinking, Magnetism,
Filtering, Mixtures, Separating Mixtures, Recycling,
Liquids, Solids, Dissolving

Themes
Matter, Scale, Stability

Mathematics Strands
Number, Statistics, Measurement,
Discrete Mathematics, Logic and Language

Nature of Science and Mathematics
Real-Life Applications, Science and Technology

Time
Three to six weeks of small-group learning station activities,
culminating in a one-hour, whole-class activity

by
Laura Lowell and Carolyn Willard

LHS GEMS

Great Explorations in Math and Science
Lawrence Hall of Science
University of California at Berkeley

Cover Design
Carol Bevilacqua

Illustrations
Lisa Klofkorn

Photographs
Richard Hoyt
Laurence Bradley

Lawrence Hall of Science, University of California, Berkeley, CA 94720-5200

Chairman: Glenn T. Seaborg
Director: Ian Carmichael

Publication of *Sifting Through Science* was made possible by a grant from the McDonnell-Douglas Employee's Community Fund and the McDonnell-Douglas Foundation. The GEMS Project and the Lawrence Hall of Science greatly appreciate this support.

Initial support for the origination and publication of the GEMS series was provided by the A.W. Mellon Foundation and the Carnegie Corporation of New York. Under a grant from the National Science Foundation, GEMS Leader's Workshops have been held across the country. GEMS has also received support from: the McDonnell-Douglas Foundation and the McDonnell-Douglas Employee's Community Fund; the Hewlett Packard Company; the people at Chevron USA; Join Hands, the Health and Safety Educational Alliance; the Microscopy Society of America (MSA); and the Shell Oil Company Foundation. GEMS also gratefully acknowledges the contribution of word processing equipment from Apple Computer, Inc. This support does not imply responsibility for statements or views expressed in publications of the GEMS program. For further information on GEMS leadership opportunities, or to receive a catalog and the *GEMS Network News*, please contact GEMS at the address and phone number below. We also welcome letters to the *GEMS Network News*.

International Standard Book Number: 0-924886-46-3

COMMENTS WELCOME !

Great Explorations in Math and Science (GEMS) is an ongoing curriculum development project. GEMS guides are revised periodically, to incorporate teacher comments and new approaches. We welcome your criticisms, suggestions, helpful hints, and any anecdotes about your experience presenting GEMS activities. Your suggestions will be reviewed each time a GEMS guide is revised. Please send your comments to: GEMS Revisions; University of California,Berkeley; GEMS; Lawrence Hall of Science #5200; Berkeley, CA 94720-5200. The phone number is (510) 642-7771. The fax number is (510) 643-0309.

Great Explorations in Math and Science (GEMS) Program

The Lawrence Hall of Science (LHS) is a public science center on the University of California at Berkeley campus. LHS offers a full program of activities for the public, including workshops and classes, exhibits, films, lectures, and special events. LHS is also a center for teacher education and curriculum research and development.

Over the years, LHS staff have developed a multitude of activities, assembly programs, classes, and interactive exhibits. These programs have proven to be successful at the Hall and should be useful to schools, other science centers, museums, and community groups. A number of these guided-discovery activities have been published under the Great Explorations in Math and Science (GEMS) title, after an extensive refinement and adaptation process that includes classroom testing of trial versions, modifications to ensure the use of easy-to-obtain materials, with carefully written and edited step-by-step instructions and background information to allow presentation by teachers without special background in mathematics or science.

Staff

Principal Investigator: Glenn T. Seaborg
Director: Jacqueline Barber
Associate Director: Kimi Hosoume
Associate Director/
Principal Editor: Lincoln Bergman
Science Curriculum Specialist: Cary Sneider
Mathematics Curriculum Specialist: Jaine Kopp
GEMS Network Director: Carolyn Willard
GEMS Workshop Coordinator: Laura Tucker
Staff Development Specialists: Lynn Barakos, Katharine Barrett, Kevin Beals, Ellen Blinderman, Beatrice Boffen, Gigi Dornfest, John Erickson, Stan Fukunaga, Philip Gonsalves, Cathy Larripa, Linda Lipner, Debra Sutter

Administrative Coordinator: Cynthia Eaton
Distribution Coordinator: Karen Milligan
Workshop Administrator: Terry Cort
Materials Manager: Vivian Tong
Distribution Representative: Felicia Roston
Shipping Assistants: Ben Arreguy, Bryan Burd
GEMS Marketing and Promotion Director: Gerri Ginsburg
Senior Editor: Carl Babcock
Editor: Florence Stone
Principal Publications Coordinator: Kay Fairwell
Art Director: Lisa Haderlie Baker
Designers: Carol Bevilacqua, Rose Craig, Lisa Klofkorn
Staff Assistants: Kasia Bukowinski, Larry Gates, Steve Lim, Nancy Lin, Jim Orosco, Christine Tong

Contributing Authors

Jacqueline Barber
Katharine Barrett
Kevin Beals
Lincoln Bergman
Beverly Braxton
Kevin Cuff
Linda De Lucchi
Gigi Dornfest

Jean Echols
John Erickson
Philip Gonsalves
Jan M. Goodman
Alan Gould
Catherine Halversen
Kimi Hosoume
Susan Jagoda

Jaine Kopp
Linda Lipner
Larry Malone
Cary I. Sneider
Craig Strang
Debra Sutter
Jennifer Meux White
Carolyn Willard

Reviewers

We would like to thank the following educators who reviewed, tested, or coordinated the reviewing of *this series* of GEMS materials in manuscript and draft form (including the GEMS guides *Learning About Learning, On Sandy Shores, Secret Formulas,* and *Sifting Through Science*). Their critical comments and recommendations, based on classroom presentation of these activities nationwide, contributed significantly to these GEMS publications. Their participation in the review process does not necessarily imply endorsement of the GEMS program or responsibility for statements or views expressed. This role is an invaluable one; feedback is carefully recorded and integrated as appropriate into the publications. **THANK YOU!**

ALASKA
Iditarod Elementary School, Wasilla
Tacy Carr
Cynthia Dolmas Curran
Carol Lowery
Bonnie Tesar

ARIZONA
Hualapai Elementary School, Kingman
Nora Brown
Catherine Ann Claes
Traci A. D'Arcy
Rhonda Gilbert
Lisa Julle
Barbara McLarty
Stephanie L. Murillo
Rose Roberts

Northern Arizona University, Flagstaff
Lynda Hatch

Show Low Primary School, Show Low
Lannie Gillespie
Claire Hart
Lorena Marchant*
Janice Shearer

CALIFORNIA
Albany Middle School, Albany
Jenny Anderson
Chiyo Masuda
Kay Sorg
Janet Teel

Alexandria School, Los Angeles
Manuel Basurto
Emilia Casillas
Beatriz Franco
Sandy Isomoto*

Anna Yates Elementary School, Emeryville
Aron Cargo*
Cecile L. Carraway
Sally Gallinger
Peggy Jones

Beacon Day School, Oakland
Deborah Ellis

Berkeley Arts Magnet, Berkeley
Sam Frankel
David Freedman*
Sandra Guerra
Janice Kohler

Claremont Middle School, Oakland
Susan Cristancho
Malia Dinell-Schwartz
Sheila Lucia
Mike Predovic

Cleveland Elementary School, Oakland
Cathy Chan
Jan Greer
Vivian Lura*
Patti MacFarland
Kathy Wong

Cornerstone Children's Center, Berkeley
Barbara Cottle*
Toyiu Lesoch
Anita White

Dover Middle School, Fairfield
Rebecca Hammond
Sarah Yourd

Fairmont Elementary School, El Cerrito
Nancy Buckingham
Carrie Cook
Karen DeTore
Sandi Healy
Linda Lambie
Katy Miles
Laura Peck
Nancy Rutter-Spriggs

Foshay Learning Center, Los Angeles
Stephanie Hoffman

Golden State Middle School, West Sacramento
Natasha Lowrie

Jefferson Elementary School, Berkeley
Mary Ann Furuichi
Linda Mengel
Fern Stroud
Gaye Ying

John Muir Elementary School, Berkeley
Anne Wihera Donaker*
Kathleen Giustino
Julie Koehler
Molly Shaw

Lafayette Elementary School, Oakland
Barbara B. Anderson*
Sue Capps
Veronica Rivers
Eleanor Tyson

Malcolm X Intermediate School, Berkeley
Arden Clute
DeEtte LaRue
Mahalia Ryba

Marina Middle School, Los Angeles
Leticia Escajeda

Markham Elementary School, Oakland
Eleanor Feuille
Sharon Kerr
Ruth Quezada
Audry Taylor
Margaret Wright

Moffett Elementary School, Huntington Beach
Patsy Almeida*
Mary Green
Nancy Hanan
Georgie Williams

Monlux Math/Science Center, North Hollywood
Nonnie Korten**

Nelson Elementary School, Pinedale
Julia Hollenbeck
Vicki Jackson
Erla Stanley
Phyllis Todd

Nobel Middle School, Northridge
Margie Hickman

Oxford School, Berkeley
Anita Baker*
Joe Brulenski
Barbara Edwards
Robin Gorton
Judy Kono
Carole Simmons

Park Day School, Oakland
Aggie Brenneman
Karen Corzan
Michelle McAfee Krueger
Suzie McLean-Balderston

Parker Elementary School, Oakland
Lorynne Dupree
Linda Rogers
Zerita Sharp
Marian Wilson

Sequoia Elementary School, Oakland
Lorraine Holmstedt
Pam Weber*
Naomi Williams
Cindy Young

Thousand Oaks Elementary School, Berkeley
Ray Adams*
Liz Fuentes
Maria Rosa G-Keys
Constance Jubb
Sharon Strachan
Pat Wong
Mario Zelaya

Walnut Acres Elementary School, Walnut Creek
Linda Campopiano
Maryann Connolly
Jane Erdiakoff
Linda Petrich*
Diane Provost

Washington Irving Middle School, Los Angeles
Mary Lu Camacho
Bernadette J. Cullen
Joe Kevany
Thomas Yee

Willard Junior High School, Berkeley
Kathy Evan
Clydine James

Yuk Yau Child Development Center, Oakland
Anne Marie Adams
Allison Chen*
Ivy Wong

COLORADO
Franklin Elementary School, Sterling
Vickie Baseggio
Marty Belknap
Barbara Nelson
Shelly Stumpf

Hotchkiss Elementary School, Hotchkiss
Roy Cranor
Kevin Elisha*
Sheryl Farmer
Margie Hollembeak
Becky Ruby

DISTRICT OF COLUMBIA
Anne Beers Elementary School
Elizabeth Dortch
Fredric Hutchinson
Gloria McKenzie-Freeman
Connie Parker
Gregory Taylor
Gloria Warren Tucker

Park View Elementary School
Olive Allen
Carol R. Corry
Michelle Davis
Barry G. Sprague*
Mary P. Tunstall

FLORIDA
Altamonte Elementary School, Altamonte Springs
Nancy Wileden

Seminole County Public Schools, Sanford
Beth Farina**

INDIANA
Indian Creek Elementary School, Indianapolis
Jill Bless
Monica Ellis*
Jennifer Hicks
Kent Jackson
Amy Tippett

IOWA

GMG Elementary School, Green Mountain
Nadine McLaughlin*
Todd Schuster
Catherine Vint
Lynne Wallace

MAINE

Coastal Ridge Elementary School, York
Nancy Annis
Rick Comeau
Julie Crafts
Patricia Gray
Carol A. Moody

York Middle School, York
Andrew Berenson
Deborah J. Bradburn
Rick Comeau
Jean Dominguez
Susan E. Miller
Robert G. Vincent

MICHIGAN

Marine City Middle School, Marine City
Peggy Brooks
Gina Day
Laura Newton
Alan Starkey

NEW JERSEY

Evergreen School, Scotch Plains
Laura Agnostak
Antoinette Fahrmann
Patricia McFall
Lynn Sanders
Marilyn Tucker

Fairleigh Dickinson University, Madison
Henry Gary**

NORTH CAROLINA

C.W. Stanford Middle School, Hillsborough
Leslie Kay Jones
Tom Kuntzleman
Christopher Longwill
Dawn M. Wills

Grady Brown Elementary School, Hillsborough
Lisa A. Crocker
Audrey T. Johnson
Sandra Kosik
Sandra L. McKee
Tonya L. Price
Karen Sexton

OREGON

Whitman Elementary, Portland
Dawn Dzubay
Saundra Liberator
Marianne McClenaghan
Linda O'Toole*
Barbara Pavlicek
Beth Tate

WASHINGTON

Orchards Elementary School, Vancouver
Mary Jane Boyle
Debbie Doden
Heidi Graumann*
Debra Palmer
Fay Stewart

WEST VIRGINIA

Flinn Elementary School, Charleston
Sharon Adkins
Ann B. Edele
Kathy Kemper
Louise St. Clair

*On-Site Coordinator for *Sifting Through Science*
**Regional Trial Test Coordinator for *Sifting Through Science*

Acknowledgments

The activities in this guide derive from a multitude of different activities that have been presented to young students at the Lawrence Hall of Science (LHS) for many years. In particular, many past and present staff members of the LHS Chemistry Department have sifted through these activities in their own ways. A popular class entitled "Stirring Up Science" provided the initial inspiration for this guide, which, as it evolved during development and classroom testing, wound up being more about "sifting" than "stirring!"

The authors would like to thank Leigh Agler, Lynn Barakos, Kevin Beals, Anne Brocchini, Jennifer Seiler, Rebecca Tilley, and all past or present Chemistry staff members. The GEMS Director, Jacqueline Barber, was instrumental in evolving the pedagogical emphases and sequence of the guide. The authors also offer a special thank you to Janet Levinson. Her class at Oxford School in Berkeley played an important role as the first classroom in which the activities were tested.

Jaine Kopp, the GEMS Mathematics Curriculum Specialist, provided major and invaluable contributions to the graphing activities. She was also instrumental in obtaining the photographs for the guide. We express our appreciation to all the students at Wilson Elementary School in San Leandro, California, who took part in the photo sessions, with very special thanks to their teacher, Sally Barry, who also appears in several of the photos.

Florence Stone, the GEMS Editor, helped gather and refine literature connections and resources. The GEMS Principal Editor, Lincoln Bergman, wrote the poems on sifting and contributed to the introduction and background sections.

Will it sink
Will it float
Is it anchor
Or a boat?
If it's rock
Will it sink?
What do you think?

Magnetic attraction
Is something unique
Whatever's attracted
By magnets we seek
If it doesn't attract
We find that out too
Wonder what makes
That invisible glue
What sort of objects
Do magnets hold?
Magnetic attraction
Mighty and bold!

Sifting sifting
Sifting sands
Through a sifter's
Criss-cross bands
Separating sand
From bean
Is the sort of sift
We mean
What comes through
We realize
Is smaller than
The sifter's size!

Garbage is sifted
To save what we can
Some is re-used
That's a good plan
Soon every child
Every Keisha and Michael
Will be happy to tell you
New ways to recycle!

Contents

Introduction

Young children are natural scientists! Children use all their senses as they eagerly explore the world around them and investigate the objects it contains. Objects need to be tested to see how they feel, if they are hard or soft, if they make a noise when they fall, if they roll, etc. All these sensory explorations reveal properties or attributes of the objects that surround the child—and this is the beginning of scientific thought.

The physical science activities in *Sifting Through Science* extend the natural curiosity of young students by providing them with objects and time for free exploration, challenges to focus further explorations, and opportunities for meaningful reflection. Throughout the unit, students engage in many of the same kinds of activities that scientists do, as they observe, predict, test, communicate, record, and apply their findings.

The unit consists of a series of three free-exploration learning stations and a concluding, whole-group activity. In each of the first three activities, a single learning station is set up for the class to visit in groups of four to six students. The three learning stations are: 1) a water tub and materials for investigation of sink/float properties; 2) magnets and a tub containing a mixture of sand and a collection of objects, both magnetic and non-magnetic; and 3) a tub containing a mixture of sand and beans, with various tools that can be used to separate the elements in the mixture.

To introduce each learning station, you gather the entire class in a rug or circle area to demonstrate the activity and convey the challenge. After all students have had ample time to freely explore the learning station activity in small groups, you convene the young scientists again as a whole class to discuss their discoveries. Graphing plays a central role in helping students interpret their findings. If there is time, you may give them further challenges at the learning station.

In the fourth activity, students are called upon to apply all of the scientific properties and processes that they have "sifted through" at the learning stations. Each student receives a "garbage dump," a cup containing salt, sand, metal, and wax. The challenge is to separate the mixture without using their hands. Students reinforce, deepen, and extend the skills and concepts learned at the three learning stations by using water to make the wax float, magnets to remove the metal, and a sifter with tiny holes to separate the sand. The connections to recycling and general care for the environment add important real-life significance to the activities. It is well worth noting that this activity is also a wonderful assessment of the skills and knowledge that students have gained at the learning station. Other opportunities for assessing student grasp of the skills and content of the unit are highlighted in the "Assessment Suggestions" section, page 76.

Mathematics is an integral part of these activities. Students graph their findings, use numbers in context, count, and refine logical thinking skills as they sort and classify objects by their properties. Younger students create real-object graphs, and older students can make both pictorial and more abstract graphs. This unit is an ideal vehicle for helping students learn the uses of graphs and how to interpret them. For more information on graphs please see the "Special Note on Graphing" on page 71.

All activities in the unit use readily available materials. The learning stations can be set up in dish tubs or at a water table or sand table if you have either of these available. "Summary Outlines" are provided on page 81 to help you guide your students through these activities. The "Literature Connections" section, page 79, lists books that make meaningful connections to these activities.

Sifting Through Science strengthens the early childhood physical science focus of the GEMS series. In response to strong teacher demand, and drawn from many exciting and effective inquiry-based activities always under development at the Lawrence Hall of Science, these activities provide your students with experiences that will help construct a foundation for future learning. Tied together by a strong real-life connection, they also provide an early opportunity for students to think about the relationship of people to the environment.

The very process of sifting is an important part of science and scientific investigation. Humanity's search over the eons to separate, compare, sort, and classify materials and objects, to learn more about smaller and smaller particles of matter, to experiment with new combinations of ingredients and see how they interact has been the driving force of much scientific exploration. The separation of mixtures, filtering out one substance from another, numerous chemical and physical separation techniques used in the laboratory, even the ability to isolate a gene or virus—all, at their most basic level, have to do with one form or another of sifting. Of course, sifting has countless other real-world applications, from sand boxes and oil filters to preparation of food and drink. When it comes to logical thinking and problem-solving skills, it is no accident that we often say we are "sifting" through a problem in our minds to find a solution! *Sifting Through Science* can help launch your students on a lifetime of understanding that the natural and fun process of sifting is a big part of science.

Language acquisition is also an important part of this unit. Given the multiplicity of languages in schools across the country it is worth noting that these activities—which involve free exploration, real-object graphing, group communication, and many opportunities for all students to draw, discuss, and write about their experiences—all lend themselves to English language acquisition. All of the learning stations in *Sifting Through Science* encourage student use of key vocabulary through exploration and descriptive observation. English language learners are further assisted by the pictorial nature of the graphs. *On Sandy Shores,* a GEMS guide for Grades 2–4, features a number of "activity structures" especially designed to foster language acquisition. You might consider applying some of these in this guide, particularly in connection with Activity 4, where students could do, for example, "Partner Parade" to communicate what they know about recycling to each other.

The activities in this unit can be presented in a flexible way, depending on your preferences and curricular emphases. It is our hope that whichever way you sift them, they will prove rewarding and memorable for you and your students. Accessible as the materials are, straightforward as the challenges may seem, we nevertheless suspect, that, long before the sifting's done, many intriguing new discoveries will be made!

One teacher told us that in the past she'd done some sinking/floating, magnet, and sifting activities, but presented them as separate activities. She loved the way this unit helped tie the discoveries and learnings together in a larger context.

More on the Learning Station Format

Why cycle students through a learning station instead of presenting a whole-class lesson? There are several advantages to the learning station format that is used in the first three activities of *Sifting Through Science*. First, it's easier for teachers to gather, prepare, and clean up materials for a single station than for a whole class. Also, since sand and water learning stations are especially exciting for students, having only one such station set up at a time makes management easier.

Another reason for the learning station format in *Sifting Through Science* is that many pre-kindergarten and early elementary teachers are already accustomed to offering a variety of activities at stations or centers, and have time built into the week for these free-choice explorations. (Some already have a sand or water table.) The learning station activities from this unit can often fit right in with "center time."

Pedagogically, the learning station format has some advantages too. It is especially well-suited to providing opportunities for open-ended exploration. Free exploration, which is central to all scientific endeavor, provides a solid foundation for more structured learning. It is critically important to provide time for students to investigate at their own level and pace. By asking focused questions, we can help students articulate a discovery, or we can add challenges to help students continue down a specific learning path. When given a chance, students will naturally engage in many of the observations and tests they need to build their understanding and widen their experience. Student exploration at the sand or water table allows them to learn some important things on their own that may be difficult to anticipate, label, or even detect at the time.

GEMS guides such as *Bubble Festival* (K–6), *Mystery Festival* (2–8), *Build It! Festival* (K–6), and *Math Around the World* (5–8) all feature the learning station format. These guides offer other ways to use learning stations, in addition to the single station format used in *Sifting Through Science*. There are many different approaches for one classroom or for a large group or whole-school festival. Varying formats and possible station selections are introduced in these guides. Some GEMS festival guides also provide whole-class lessons to deepen the science and math learning at the stations, or refer to other GEMS teacher's guides that provide opportunities for further investigations with related content.

Importantly, learning stations also can provide excellent jumping-off points for more formal, in-depth learning. For example, many teachers and students find further study of magnetism irresistible after the class has discovered its "attractions" at the learning station.

Time Frame

In each of the first three activities, a single learning station is set up for the class to visit in groups of four to six students. The time needed for the whole class to explore the activity will vary according to your schedule, class size, and how long students spend at the learning station. Most teachers find that each learning station activity needs to be available for from one to two weeks. The fourth activity, Garbage Dumps, is designed to be a single, whole class session.

Activity 1: Sink or Float?
Class Introduction...20 minutes
Learning Station Activity.....................................1–2 weeks
Class Debrief...20–45 minutes

Activity 2: Magnets
Class Introduction...20 minutes
Learning Station Activity.....................................1–2 weeks
Class Debrief...20–30 minutes

Activity 3: Sifting Sand and Beans
Class Introduction...15 minutes
Learning Station Activity.....................................1–2 weeks
Class Debrief...20–30 minutes

Activity 4: Garbage Dumps
Preparation..30 minutes
Class Activity..45 minutes

Activity 1: Sink or Float?

Overview

In this activity, a sink/float learning station is set up for small groups of students to explore. The learning station can be as simple as a couple of dish tubs filled with water or as fancy as a commercial water table. After you introduce the sink/float challenge to the whole class, the time needed for all students to visit the station will vary according to your schedule, class size, and how long students spend at the learning station. Most teachers find that the learning station activity needs to be available for from one to two weeks.

At the learning station, students act as scientists, predicting whether various objects will sink or float, then testing their predictions, and classifying the objects into two categories. Of course, students will want to do some additional, less structured explorations, too. Rest assured that what may seem like "just playing" is valuable, direct experience that can yield important lessons.

After everyone has had ample time at the learning station, the students gather as a large group, just as the scientific community does, to share their findings. Students report their observations using thumbs up or thumbs down to show whether objects sank or floated, and record their results on a large real-object graph. Older students go on to create a pictorial graph as well. Please see the "Special Note on Graphing" on page 71 for more information.

If time and circumstances permit, the students can return to the learning station. The "Going Further" activities on pages 18 and 19 are strongly recommended for older students. They provide challenges more commensurate with the abilities of first and second grade students.

Student's experiences at the learning station and in the concluding discussion give them early and positive insight into the nature of science and mathematics. The goal of this activity is **not** for students to master the principles of buoyancy, density, and displacement, but rather for them to begin to develop an intuitive understanding of these concepts, and to use science and mathematics processes to learn about the properties of a floater or sinker. Student's experiences will also contribute to their formation of basic concepts about the repeatability of results in science. (The "floater" floats every time.) Skills developed include: observing, predicting, testing, comparing, classifying, communicating, counting, estimating, and graphing.

Students get very excited by water play. Having an adult monitor the station helps to focus the students and enables them to slow down and make predictions and observations.

Preschool and kindergarten teachers need only the real-object class graph; teachers of first and second grade students will need both the real-object graph and the pictorial graph. Both of these class graphs can be used again for the other activities in this unit as well as for other graphing opportunities.

*Interested in finding out more about the intriguing question: "Why **does** a battleship float?" See the "Behind the Scenes" section, page 65.*

What You Need

For the class:
- ❏ 1 clear plastic sweater box or similar plastic container, at least 4" deep
- ❏ 1 permanent black marker (wide-tipped, if available)
- ❏ 1 roll masking tape
- ❏ 1 yardstick or meter stick
- ❏ 1 real-object graph, at least 9' long and 1' wide (see "Getting Ready Before the Day of the Activity" for details)

Note: The additional items below are needed for the pictorial graph, for first and second grade students only:
- ❏ 1 sheet of paper, any color, about 6' long and 1' wide
- ❏ about 20–25 3" x 3" post-its, all the same color **OR** paper and a glue stick
- ❏ a pencil or crayon for each pair of students

For the learning station:
- ❏ 20–25 objects for students to test in the water, about half that will sink and half that will float. (If possible, test them yourself ahead of time, since you may not always be sure of which float and which don't!) Be sure to include:
  - __ crayon that floats*
  - __ wax candle
  - __ strawberry basket
  - __ rock about 3" in diameter
  - __ ball that floats
  - __ cup with a removable lid
  - __ film canister with lid
  - __ oil-based clay
- ❏ 3 cafeteria trays
- ❏ 1 restaurant bus tub **OR** 2 standard dish tubs **OR** a water table (Whichever you use, it must be at least 6" deep.)
- ❏ water (enough to fill the tubs to about 4")
- ❏ 2 file folders
- ❏ glue
- ❏ sink and float station signs (1 each—masters on pages 20 and 21)
- ❏ 1 copy of the Activity Task Card for Volunteers (master on page 22)
- ❏ a stack of newspaper or old towels for spills
- ❏ (*optional*) a large sheet of plastic to put under the station for spills

*Note on crayons: While crayons are made mostly of wax, some crayons sink and some float! For the learning station in Activity 1, we recommend that you include only crayons that float. Knowing that wax generally floats will be important in Activity 4, when your students try to separate wax from their "garbage dumps." After the whole-class discussion in Activity 1, when you've established that wax *generally* floats, you may decide to encourage students to test a variety of crayons. Why do some crayons float while others sink? Do they contain ingredients other than wax? See "Going Further" #6, page 18.

For more on the manufacture of crayons, see the book How Is A Crayon Made? *in the "Resources" section.*

Getting Ready

Before the Day of the Activity

1. For the entire *Sifting Through Science* unit, decide on the place where you'll gather the whole class. This should be away from the materials, preferably with students seated in a circle, to introduce the learning station activities and to hold concluding discussions.

2. Your class will need time to visit the learning station in groups of about four to six students. Keeping in mind your schedule, class size, grade level, and other factors, estimate how long the station will need to be set up, and decide where it should be located.

Some teachers prefer to set up an outdoor sink/float learning station, if possible, as it minimizes the need for mopping up. For younger students or those new to water table explorations, an adult monitor is highly recommended.

3. If time allows, we strongly recommend that you plan to set up the water station *without* sink/float items for free exploration for a week before the formal sink/float intro- duction. You could provide cups, funnels, and any other items that will encourage water exploration.

4. If possible, arrange for one or more adults to monitor the learning station. Give them an idea what to expect, and make them a copy of the Activity Task Card for Volunteers (master on page 22).

5. Make one copy of each of the sink and float signs (mas- ters on pages 20 and 21) and glue each to a separate file folder. This way the signs will stand by themselves.

6. Gather the items that students will test.

It's nice to laminate the signs or cover them with contact paper, if possible, to prevent them from getting soggy.

7. Make a real-object graph:

    a. Tape a 9' x 1' sheet of vinyl, plastic, or paper to the floor so that it won't wrinkle or shift as you draw lines on it.

    b. Use a yardstick and permanent black marker to make a grid composed of 6" squares. The grid should be at least 18 squares long and two squares wide. If you use paper for the graph, it should be laminated for durability.

The real-object graph should be sturdy and re-usable. You can use butcher paper and laminate it, or use vinyl from a fabric store, or a shower curtain in solid white, clear, or pastel colors. Grid lines can be made with permanent marker, electrical tape, or other tape of contrasting color. Please see the "Resources" section, page 58, for a source of commercially made graphs.

8. **For 1st–2nd grade students ONLY!** Teachers of prekindergarten children should skip this activity. It is OPTIONAL for kindergarten, depending upon the abilities and prior experiences of the students. Make the grid for a new graph to record the real-object graph. This new graph is a pictorial graph and allows the class to save the information they gathered from their explorations.

    a. Cut or piece together a sheet of paper 72" x 12" (6' x 1'). Using a yardstick and a marker, draw lines to divide the width (12") of the paper into three 4"-wide sections.

    b. Then draw vertical lines to create two rows of 4"-square boxes. There will be 18 boxes in each row.

c. There will be a long blank row. Use this area to label the graph with your class and/or write questions that invite others to look at the data on it.

"Sink and Float Graph" Did more objects sink or float?														

d. Gather enough 3" square post-its for your class to record the real-object graph. Be sure the post-its are the same color so students can more readily focus on the data and not be distracted by the color of the post-it. If post-its are not readily available, cut 3" squares of paper—again all the same color—and gather a glue stick. Gather enough pencils or crayons for each pair of students to record their objects.

e. Make labels for the pictorial graph. On one post-it, draw two objects floating in water (similar to the sign from the station) and write the word "float" on it. On another post-it, draw two objects that sank in water (similar to the station sign) and write the word "sink" on it.

On the Day of the Activity

1. Set up the learning station: Fill the large tub (or two smaller tubs or water table) with about 4" of water. Place the items to be tested near it on a tray. Put out two additional trays. (After the whole class introduction, you'll place the sink sign near one tray, and the float sign near the other.) Put the newspaper or old towels nearby.

2. Set up your introduction area: Fill a clear sweater box with about 3" of water. Borrow three items from the learning station—one that sinks to the bottom (such as a rock), one that floats on the surface (such as a ping-pong ball), and one that floats, but does so with much of the object below the surface (such as a strawberry basket). Have the sink and float signs handy.

3. For the day you'll conclude Activity 1, plan to have handy in the discussion area: the real-object graph, the sink and float signs, the sweater box with water, and all the items tested at the learning station. For first and second grade, you'll also need the pictorial graph, post-it notes, and pencils or crayons.

Introducing Floaters to the Whole Class

1. Gather your students into a circle on the floor. Ask if anyone knows what scientists do. Accept their responses and if necessary add that scientists look carefully at things and do experiments to find out more about things. Say that everyone in the class will get a chance to do some of the same things that scientists do.

2. Hold up the object you chose that is a definite floater, such as a ping-pong ball. Ask the students to say something true about it. [it is round, white, it bounces] Point out that we don't know for sure that it will bounce by just looking at it, but we could test the ball to find out for sure. Bounce the ball for the students.

3. Ask them if they think the ball would float in your clear container of water. Say, "Show me if you think it will float by showing me a thumbs up." Then say, "Thumbs down if you think it will sink." Wait for all students to vote, then put the ball in the water and ask the students to show with their thumbs whether it floats or sinks.

4. Ask if they think it will float if you try it again. (Some of your students may not be sure.) You may want to go ahead and try it again, again asking for a thumb signal prediction and then another thumb signal to describe the result. Elicit a class definition of "floater" from the students. [Floaters are things that stay at the top of the water.] Put the ball near the float sign.

With younger students, simply begin by asking who has played with toys and objects in water before. Then ask what they think will happen when a ball is placed in water. Accept their responses then demonstrate and ask what happened. Through the discussion, assist students in acquiring vocabulary and descriptive language/concepts related to sinking and floating which they'll use as they test the objects. Later in this session, or at the end of the unit, you could discuss with younger students how what they did is what scientists do.

Introducing Sinkers to the Whole Class

1. Hold up the object you chose that is a definite sinker, such as the rock, and say, "Can you tell me something true about this rock?" Accept all their observations, helping students as appropriate to distinguish between things that can be observed and those things that might need to be tried or tested to find out.

2. Ask them to predict with their thumbs if the rock will float or sink. Put the rock in the water and ask for a show of thumbs for the result.

3. Elicit a definition of "sinkers" from the students. [Sinkers are things that stay at the bottom of the water.] Put the rock near the sink sign.

What About Things that Float Partly Underwater?

1. Hold up the object that you chose that floated partially submerged, such as the strawberry basket. Have students use thumbs to predict whether it will sink or float, then test the object.

2. Say that for now we will call this object a "floater" because it does not actually touch or stay at the bottom.

3. Review the revised class definitions: **a sinker stays on the bottom, and a floater stays off the bottom.**

Introducing the Procedure at the Learning Station

1. Tell the students that they'll get to be scientists and test lots of things to find out if they float or sink.

2. Tell them that they will get to go to the learning station in small groups. Explain the procedure:

   a. Go to the station and choose an object to test.

   b. **Predict or guess** if it will be a sinker or floater.

   c. Tell your guess to someone.

   d. Test your guess by putting the object in the water.

With younger students, the teacher or volunteers may need to help guide the steps of this process at the learning station. The emphasis in all cases still should be on student-centered exploration.

e. If it floats, put it on the tray by the float sign; if it sinks, put it on the tray by the sink sign.

3. Review the student's tasks by asking them questions like, "What do you do first?" "What next?" and so on. Send the first group of students to the station. Place the float sign near one tray at the station, and the sink sign near the other tray.

Monitoring the Learning Station

1. **Allow students plenty of time to freely explore at the learning station.** Make sure everyone has at least one chance to visit the station.

2. If another adult will be assisting, explain the open-ended, discovery nature of the activity, and give them a copy of the Activity Task Card for Volunteers. You or whoever monitors the station should:

- Remind students to predict before testing.

- Make sure that everyone tests the wax candle and crayon; they will need to know that wax floats for a later activity.

- Resist the temptation to give explanations.

- Periodically put objects that have been placed on both the sink and float trays back onto the original tray for more students to test.

- Toss a section of newspaper or towel on the floor to absorb spills if the floor gets too wet.

- Ask questions such as, "Is that what you thought would happen?" "Did any of the objects do something different than what you guessed?"

- Assess your students' progress. Glance at the trays and observe the objects placed there. Are they placed according to whether or not they floated? Observe the students. Are the students able to predict and then test?

Discussing the Learning Station

Getting Ready

1. Bring over the tray of objects they tested, the clear sweater box filled with water, and the sink and float signs.

2. Place the real-object graph on the floor in the middle of the discussion area.

For older students only:

3. Post the paper pictorial graph on the wall in the discussion area where students will be able to see it.

4. Bring a post-it note and a pencil or crayon for each pair of students, two extra post-its and a pencil or crayon for yourself, plus the sink/float post-its made before class.

Introducing the Real-Object Graph

1. After all students have had ample time to visit the learning station, gather the students in a circle around the real-object graph.

2. Put the float sign at the head of one row, and explain that objects that float will be put in that row. Say that sinkers will go in the other row (put the sink sign at the head of the adjacent row).

3. Ask the students to raise their hand if they tested the wax birthday candle. Ask for a show of thumbs if it floated (thumbs up) or sank (thumbs down). If there is disagreement, test the candle by putting it into the clear container of water.

Depending on the size of your group and grade level, you may decide to give an object to each student, rather than to each pair. The advantage of course is more individual involvement, but the challenge is to keep the graphing moving at a quick but understandable pace.

If you run out of squares on the graph, just have students place objects on the floor in approximately the position they'd be in if the grid continued.

One teacher said, "My students had some interesting discussions, because a child or two would comment that big things sink. But watermelons and pumpkins float! We talked about ocean liners, too."

4. Put the candle in the first square of the graph in the row headed by the float sign.

5. Repeat with an object that sank, placing it on the graph.

Placing Objects on the Graph

1. Hand out objects that the students have tested, one to every *pair* of students around the circle. Tell them that they will work with a partner—one person holds the object and the other places the object on the graph.

2. Point to the first object held by a student and ask the class to show with their thumb whether the object is a floater or a sinker.

3. Have the student who didn't get to hold the object place it in the correct row of the graph. If there is a split vote on an object, allow that student to re-test the object in the clear container, and then place it on the graph.

4. After about six or seven objects have been placed on the graph, stop and ask, "What do you notice about the graph?" Listen to their observations.

5. Focus on some questions to encourage mathematical thinking: How many sinkers are there? How many floaters? Are there more floaters or sinkers so far? Show the students how to pair each object in the "float" row with the adjacent one in the "sink" row. You can call these "partners." Then, together, count the objects without "partners." How many more sinkers (or floaters) are there?"

6. Ask if they think there will still be more sinkers than floaters (or vice versa, depending on what the graph shows) when all the objects are on the graph.

7. When all objects have been placed, ask, "How many sinkers?" "How many floaters?" "Are there more floaters or sinkers?" "How many more?" "From looking at our graph, what are your ideas about sinkers?" "Floaters?" "Is there anything the same about all floaters/sinkers?" "What surprised you?" Accept all answers.

Creating a Pictorial Graph (for first and second grade students only)

1. Tell students that you can't leave the graph with sinkers and floaters in the middle of the floor for very long. One good way to record and remember the results is to make a picture graph on paper to post on the wall. Then the class will have a record of their findings they can discuss and share with others. (Don't take apart the real-object graph yet.)

2. Explain that the first step in making this graph will be for students to draw a picture of their objects. Each pair should work together to draw the object they placed on the real-object graph. You could either pass out a crayon and post-it note to each pair and have them draw right there at the circle, or you could send them back to tables or desks to draw. Older students can label their drawings.

You could model this task for students by drawing the candle on a post-it before they start drawing.

3. Emphasize that it is fine if their drawing does not look exactly like the object—they can make rough sketches. While they are drawing, you'll need to draw two pictures on post-it notes—one of the wax birthday candle you put in the first "floater" square, and one of the object you placed in the first "sinker" square.

4. After they have drawn their objects, refocus the group's attention. Using the sink/float post-its that you made before class, label the rows of the pictorial graph, in the same way as the real-object graph.

5. Show students the picture you drew of the birthday candle. Ask them where you should put this picture. Stick the post-it note in the top square of the "float" row. Do the same with your picture of the sinker.

It is not necessary to place the picture in the same relative square as the items on the real-object graph, but it does need to be in the correct row.

6. Have students raise their hands if they are holding a picture of a floater. Have them come and stick their post-it note pictures on the graph. Do the same with the pictures of the sinkers.

7. Encourage the class to reflect on the pictorial graph and compare it to the one with real objects on it. How is it the same as the graph of real objects? How is it different? (You may want to count the sinkers and floaters again on each of the graphs. Even if the order of specific items changes, the number remains constant. Are there more sinkers? floaters?)

8. If time and circumstances permit, leave the water table up, and give your students some of the challenges in the "Going Further" section. Otherwise, dismantle the water learning station and real-object graph, leave up the pictorial graph, and go on to Activity 2.

Going Further

1. Challenge the students to develop tricks to turn a sinker into a floater and vice versa. You might even challenge them to find a way to make *all* the objects float (or sink) by combining them with other objects or changing them in some way.

2. Invite students to bring items from home to test (have them check with a parent to be sure the object can get wet). Limit the size of objects they bring in by giving them a square of paper to help them remember the maximum size that will fit on the real-object graph. Older students might want to make their own graphs in journals or on grid paper and write two sentences about their graphs.

3. You'll find that students will have many creative ideas to pursue, and they will want to share further discoveries with the class. If possible, schedule another class sharing time. You could help the class articulate and illustrate a story ("Sink or Float?") on the chalkboard or in a class book about what floated, what did not, and about their other investigations and discoveries.

4. If students have begun to write, you could encourage them to write several sentences with illustrations in a journal about their experience at the sink/float station. Older students could write a response to the question: "Why do some things float and others don't?"

5. Encourage students to do experiments in the bathtub at home to find sinkers and floaters.

6. Have the class gather a variety of different brands and colors of crayons to test. Have them investigate and record on the real-object graph which sink and which float. Students could be asked why they think some float/sink, and older students could even write to crayon companies to ask about how their crayons are made. (Also, see the book *How Is A Crayon Made?* in the "Resources" section.) As another exploration, have students try crayons both with and without paper wrapping.

An interesting sink/float demonstration can be done with M&Ms. Drop an M&M (the red ones work well) "M" side up into a clear container of room temperature water. The candy will sink. In a few minutes the candy coating will dissolve and the "M" will slide off and eventually float to the surface (a gentle stirring may be needed to separate the "M" from bits of candy coating). Ask your students why they think the "M" floats [it's made of wax!]

7. Do all soaps float? Do all metals sink? How about different types of wood? Test a variety of other objects made out of the same material. What about objects that can either sink or float, depending on other factors—clay sinks as a ball, but floats when made into a boat; a cup with a lid can either float or sink; etc.

Older students may be interested in the story of how floating soap was first made. In 1878, Proctor and Gamble Company developed a high-quality soap called "White Soap." One day a factory production supervisor went to lunch and forgot to turn off the mixing solution. As a result more air than usual was whipped into the soapy solution. Rather than throw away the mixture, it was placed into hardening frames to make bars of soap. Then it was discovered that because of the air whipped into the soap, the soap bars floated! Consumer reaction was so favorable that the company ordered all their soap to have air mixed into it. Soon that soap would be named "Ivory."

sink

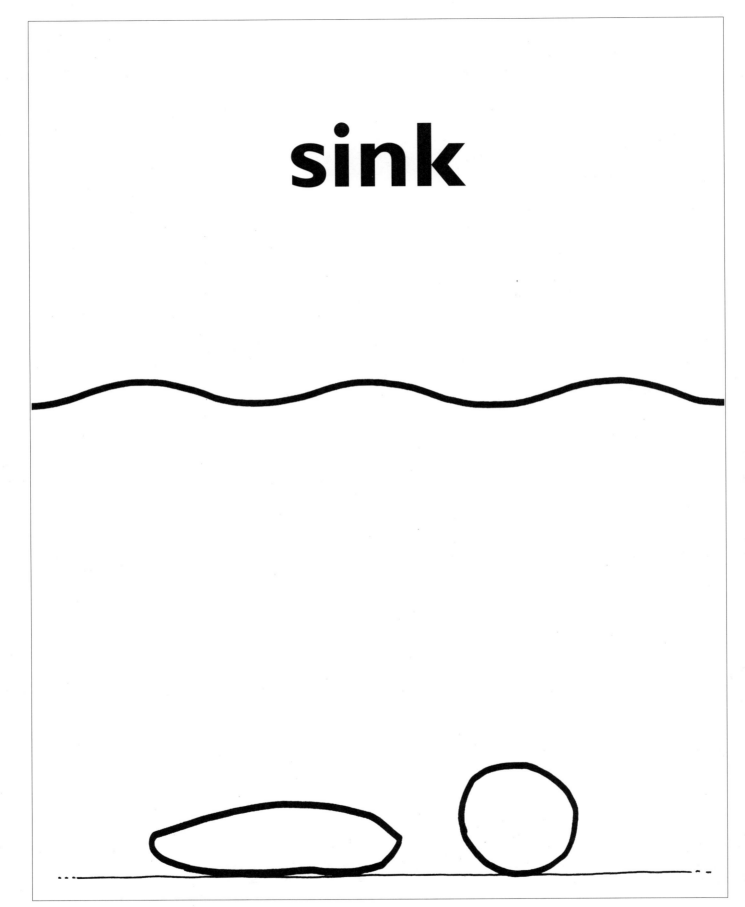

float

Sink or Float?

Activity Task Card for Volunteers

Your goal is to assist the students in making their own discoveries, while keeping the activity safe, and the mess under control. As needed, remind students of the challenge, but refrain from demonstrating how it is done. Here's what the students are to do:

- Choose an object.
- Predict whether it will sink or float. Tell someone your prediction.
- Test it in the water.
- Place the object on the appropriate sink or float tray.

As students explore, ask open-ended questions, such as:

- What have you discovered?
- What's happening to the object? Is that what you thought would happen?
- Did any of the objects do something different than what you guessed?
- What surprised you?

If students get involved in explorations unrelated to sinking and floating, you might want to steer them gently back on task. Make sure to intervene if you see an unsafe behavior. However, keep in mind that what may appear as "fooling around" can lead to some of the deepest learning experiences. Some of the greatest scientific discoveries have been made when scientists freely and creatively explored and imagined!

Young students need ample time to explore and work with the materials before tackling more structured challenges. Resist the temptation to give explanations to students. Your main role is to keep the station stocked and ready for more students to freely explore it.

Tips for Managing the Station

- If necessary, remind students of the class definitions:

  sinkers: things that stay on the bottom of the water
  floaters: things that stay *off* the bottom of the water (Things that float suspended in the middle of the water should be called floaters.)

- Make sure that everyone tests the **wax candle** and **crayon;** they will need to know that wax floats for a later activity.

- Periodically put objects back on the original tray for more students to test.

- Toss a section of newspaper or towel on the floor to absorb spills if the floor gets too wet.

- Encourage each group to help clean up for the next group.

Activity 2: Magnets

Overview

This activity follows the same format as the sink/float activity, but this time the students will find that the learning station is full of sand. Their challenge is to use magnets to test objects they find in the sand to see if they are magnetic or non-magnetic.

Before visiting the learning station, the students generate a list of things they know or have heard about magnets. During the concluding whole-group discussion, students discuss their discoveries, then graph objects they gather from around the room as either magnetic or non-magnetic. After comparing the two groups, the students make generalizations about things that stick to magnets.

Among science concepts explored are: repeatability of results; mixtures and separating mixtures; the idea that objects can be described; the property of magnetic/non-magnetic; and the idea that magnets can be used as tools to attract (and sort) magnetic from non-magnetic things. Students gain important experience with the fascinating phenomenon of magnetism. As in the sink/float activity, the concepts and techniques gained at the learning station will be applied in Activity 4 when the students become "garbage recycling scientists."

Skills developed in this activity include: observing, predicting, testing, sorting, comparing, classifying, communicating, counting, estimating, graphing, and drawing conclusions. Students increase their understanding of how numbers can be used to tell about things, and how graphs can represent what we find out about the properties of objects.

The goals of this activity are to explore how magnets work, to begin to classify objects by whether or not they are magnetic, and to build toward separating metals from a mixture in the later whole-class activity. While these magnet explorations are not meant to be a unit on magnetism, the further study of magnets can be a very rich and fascinating accompaniment to Sifting Through Science. *For ideas on pursuing the study of magnets, please see "Going Further" on page 32 and the "Resources" section on page 58.*

What You Need

For the class:
- ❐ 16–32 magnets, including at least 8 magnets that are bigger than 1"
  NOTE: You'll need 8 to 12 of the magnets for the learning station. In the concluding activity, you'll need one per student, or you can get by with one magnet for each pair of students if necessary.*
- ❐ the real-object graph from Activity 1
- ❐ broom and dust pan
- ❐ a chalkboard or large piece of paper that can be saved

For the learning station:
- ❐ 30 objects for students to test with magnets, at least half should be magnetic and half non-magnetic. Be sure to include several pieces of paper, plastic, wood, and wax (including birthday candles), paper clips, and a metal spoon. Use only a couple of metal items which do NOT stick to magnets, such as an aluminum can and a piece of aluminum foil.
- ❐ 2 cafeteria trays
- ❐ 1 restaurant bus tub **OR** 2 standard dish tubs **OR** a sand table
- ❐ sand (enough to fill the tubs to about 4")**
- ❐ 2 file folders
- ❐ glue
- ❐ magnetic and not-magnetic station signs (1 each—masters on pages 33 and 34)
- ❐ 1 copy of the Activity Task Card for Volunteers (master on page 35)
- ❐ (optional) a tarp to put under the sand table

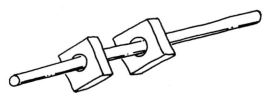

Many small magnets have a hole in the middle. Some teachers like to make a few straws available that will fit in the holes. Students who thread two magnets onto a straw will probably make some fascinating discoveries about attraction and repulsion.

*Notes about magnets: Having a variety of shapes and sizes of magnets at the station is desirable. If you put out enough magnets at the station for each student to have two, students are more likely to make discoveries about attraction and repulsion. However, providing more than two magnets per student may result in students focusing on the magnets themselves, not on the challenge of testing objects with them.

**Notes about sand: The same sand will be re-used for the learning station in Activity 3. Before buying or gathering sand, check to see if the kind you're considering gives off a dusty powder that gets into the air. If nothing else is available, slight misting may help lessen the dust. Sand makes the magnet station more interesting, but it isn't essential. You could substitute rice or corn meal for sand, or even have just the objects and the magnets.

Getting Ready

Before the Day of the Activity

1. We strongly suggest that you set up the learning station with sand for free exploration for a week before the formal introduction of the magnet activity. Add cups, strawberry baskets, funnels, and anything that will encourage sand exploration.

2. If possible, arrange for an adult to monitor the learning station. Give them an idea of what to expect (see "Monitoring the Learning Station," page 29), and make them a copy of the Activity Task Card for Volunteers (master on page 35).

3. Make one copy of each of the magnetic and not-magnetic signs (masters on pages 33 and 34) and glue each sign to a separate file folder.

4. Gather the items that the students will test.

5. Obtain enough magnets for each student to have one, and put a variety of eight to 12 of them at the learning station. Keep the rest in reserve for the whole-class magnet activity that will happen during the concluding discussion.

On the Day of the Activity

1. Set up the learning station: Fill the tubs or sand table with about 4" of sand. Set the trays near the tubs. (After the whole class introduction, you'll place the magnetic sign near one tray, and the not-magnetic sign near the other.) Mix the objects to be tested into the sand.

2. Set up your introduction area: Borrow and have handy several items from the learning station: a magnet, the magnetic and not-magnetic signs, a scrap of paper, and something that will be attracted to a magnet, such as a spoon. Post a large piece of paper to record the students' ideas about magnets, or reserve a part of the chalkboard. Entitle the paper, or write on the chalkboard, "What We Know About Magnets."

3. For the day when you wrap up Activity 2, plan to have in the discussion area: the real-object graph, the magnetic and not-magnetic signs, a magnet for yourself, a paper clip, a crayon, and enough magnets for each student in the class to have one.

Introducing Magnets

1. Gather your students in the discussion area. Ask, "What do you know or have you heard about magnets?" Accept all responses, and record them on the chalkboard or large piece of paper. (You can use this list as a pre-assessment of what the class knows about magnets. You may want to refer to or have the class refine the list at the end of the activity and/or at the end of the unit.)

2. Hold up a magnet and tell them that they will be able to use a magnet at the learning station. Ask them to show thumbs up if they think a piece of paper will stick to a magnet. Try it and have the students show thumbs down because the magnet did not stick to the paper.

3. What about a spoon? Ask students for a thumbs up/ down prediction. Hand the magnet and metal spoon to a student to try (it sticks). Have everyone show thumbs up.

4. Tell them that now there is sand at the learning station, with all sorts of things mixed in the sand. They have the chance to be magnet scientists.

Introducing the Procedure at the Learning Station

1. Tell the students that they'll test the objects in the sand to find out which ones stick to magnets.

2. If something sticks, they should take it out of the tub and put it on the tray that is near the sign that says "magnetic." Explain that magnetic means that it *sticks* to a magnet.

Note: Some students may think that if a magnet did stick, but wasn't strong enough to lift a large object, then that object should be classified as "not-magnetic." You may want to clarify that if it sticks **at all,** it's magnetic.

3. Ask, "What if an object does not stick to the magnet at all?" [They will put it near the sign that says "not-magnetic."] Place the magnetic sign near one tray at the station, and the not-magnetic sign near the other tray.

Monitoring the Learning Station

1. Make sure everyone has time to freely explore the station.

2. If another adult will be assisting, explain the open-ended, discovery nature of the activity, and give them a copy of the Activity Task Card for Volunteers. You or whoever monitors the station should:

- Remind students that objects are considered magnetic even if they only stick to the magnet a little bit.

- Ask questions such as, "Did any of the objects you tested with the magnet surprise you?" "Why?"

- When appropriate, encourage students to predict before testing objects.

- Periodically put objects that have been sorted onto the trays back into the sand.

- Sweep up sand from the floor.

- Assess student progress. Glance at the trays and observe the objects placed there. Are they placed according to whether or not they're magnetic?

3. When the magnet learning station is no longer needed, remove the objects, signs, and magnets, but leave the sand in the tubs for Activity 3. A magnet and a sifter with big holes are useful to clean out the objects from the sand. Save all the magnets for Activity 4.

Because magnets are so "attractive" to students, some of your students may be tempted to keep them. You may want to discuss budgetary realities, and how important it is to leave magnets at the station for other students to use. You might also tell students about a local store where they can buy magnets for themselves inexpensively.

One teacher dealt with the problem of magnets "disappearing" into pockets by tracing each magnet on a box lid so the students could check to see if all the magnets were at the station. It helped!

Concluding Activities

Re-Introducing the Real-Object Graph

1. After all students have worked at the learning station, gather the class in the discussion area around the real-object graph. Have on hand a magnet, a paper clip, a crayon, and the magnetic/not-magnetic signs. Place the signs at the head of each row of the real-object graph.

2. Ask, "What happened when you placed the magnet near the objects in the sand?" Encourage students to briefly share their experiences.

3. Show the paper clip to the students. Ask them to raise their hand if they tested a paper clip. Ask them to show thumbs up if the paper clip stuck to a magnet; thumbs down if it did not. Use a magnet to test it again.

4. Tell them that since it stuck to a magnet, you'll place it in the first box of the row headed by the magnetic sign.

Younger students might benefit from repeating the procedure of making the real-object graph with items they tested at the station. For younger students the testing and graphing of other objects in the room could be a "going further" activity.

5. Ask them about the crayon. Demonstrate that it doesn't stick to a magnet. Place it in the first square in the next row headed by the not-magnetic sign.

Testing and Graphing More Objects in the Room

1. Tell the students that they will each get a magnet (or one per pair) and they will go around the room and test many things in the room to see what's magnetic.

2. Set firm guidelines: Students should stay with their partners. When they see or hear your pre-arranged signal (lights on and off, a bell, or whatever signal you usually use), they must stop moving and listen. **Caution them to keep magnets away from computers, because magnets can damage them.** Send students off in pairs to explore.

3. After a few minutes, use your signal to regain students' attention. Invite the pairs of students to bring one item back to the discussion area. The object must be the size of one hand or smaller, and can either stick to a magnet or not. If they have any questions about whether or not it is okay to bring a certain object, they can raise their hands and you will come over and check it out.

4. As each pair returns to the discussion area, have them take turns holding up their items, one at a time. Have

other students predict whether or not each object is magnetic. Then have partners place their object on the graph, in the appropriate row.

5. If very few students choose non-magnetic items, choose a few yourself, and add them to the graph.

Discussing the Graph and Generalizing about Magnets

1. As you did with the sink/float graph, encourage students to interpret the graph by asking: "How many things are magnetic?" "How many are not-magnetic?" "Are there more magnetic things or not-magnetic things?" "How many more magnetic things are there than not-magnetic ones?"

2. Explain that graphs can help people understand things better. You may want to mention to older students that scientists and mathematicians often use graphs to help them organize information and find out more about things.

3. Focus the attention of the class on the row of magnetic objects. Ask, "What can you tell me about things that stick to magnets?" If they have difficulty, you may want to give them a silly example, such as: "All yellow things stick to magnets." Ask if that is true.

4. Have students look at the entire graph and try to notice something that seems to be true from what the graph shows. [things made of paper or wood aren't magnetic, plastic isn't, metal things often are…]

5. If students say that all metal is magnetic, help them modify their statement to include their experiences with aluminum foil or cans. ["*most* kinds of metal are magnetic" or "lots of metal things are magnetic, but aluminum isn't"]

6. Ask how they could find out more about which kinds of metal are magnetic. [try a lot of different metal things, observe closely, and make a graph; read books to see what other scientists have found out]

7. Refer back to the "What We Know About Magnets" list and read it to the students. Ask them if they would like to change or add anything to the list based on their investigations. Tell students they've been great magnet scientists and mathematicians.

Some teachers assign the pairs of students to find two items: one magnetic and one non-magnetic.

Another teacher said it was great finding magnetic things outside.

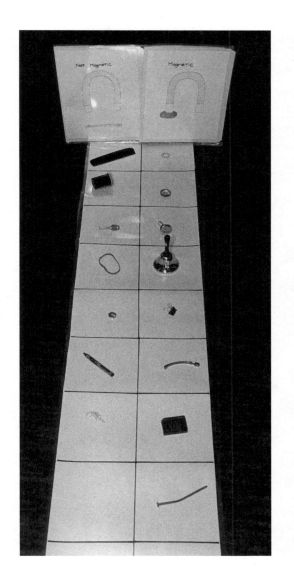

8. If time and circumstances permit, give your students some of the "Going Further" challenges below. (Some of the challenges don't require the sand learning station.)

Going Further

1. Students will be eager to share the results of their ongoing investigations. If possible, schedule more class sharing time. If students have started writing, encourage brief journal writing with illustrations. Older students could make a list of magnetic objects, write a report on "What I Learned About Magnets," or write their own responses to questions such as, "Why do you think some things are attracted by magnets and some are not?"

2. As was done in Activity 1, consider making a class pictorial graph to record student findings about magnetic and non-magnetic objects. Older students can make individual pictorial graphs from the class graph or to represent further magnet investigations of their own.

3. Challenge students to be inventors and discover ways to make magnets stick to paper or to any other object that did not stick to the magnet at first.

4. Have each student take a magnet (or magnetic craft tape) home to test objects, predicting first. (Remind them not to put the magnets near computers.) Ask them to look on their refrigerators and record any magnets on it by drawing a picture and/or describing them in words.

5. How many paper clips can hang off a magnet in a single chain without any falling off? They can try using different magnets or multiple magnets to see how that affects the chain.

6. Encourage students to conduct an investigation of metal objects. They could gather many different metal objects, test them, and graph them as to whether they are magnetic or not-magnetic. What did they find out? Can they discover a rule for metals that are magnetic?

7. Why did some parts of the sand stick to magnets? Is it metal?

8. Have students use two magnets to investigate attraction and repulsion.

magnetic

not-magnetic

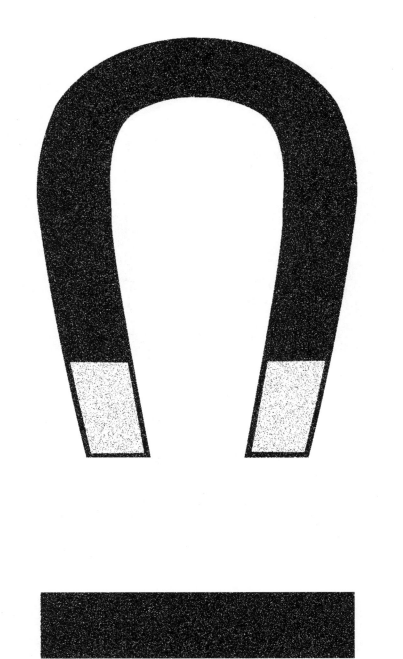

Magnets

Activity Task Card for Volunteers

Your goal is to assist the students in making their own discoveries, while keeping the activity safe, and the mess under control. As needed, remind students of the challenge, but refrain from demonstrating how it is done. Here's what the students are to do:

- Find an object.
- Test it with a magnet.
- Place the object on the appropriate tray.

As students experiment with different objects, encourage them to predict if they will stick to a magnet or not. Ask open-ended questions, such as:

- What have you discovered?
- What's happening to the object? Is that what you thought would happen?
- Did any of the objects do something different than what you guessed?
- What surprised you?

If students get involved in explorations unrelated to the challenge, you might want to steer them gently back on task. Make sure to intervene if you see an unsafe behavior. However, keep in mind that what may appear as "fooling around" can lead to some of the deepest learning experiences. Some of the greatest scientific discoveries have been made when scientists freely and creatively explored and imagined!

Young students need ample time to explore and work with the materials before tackling more structured challenges. Resist the temptation to give explanations to students. Your main role is to keep the station stocked and ready for more students to freely explore it.

Tips for Managing the Station

- If necessary, remind students of the class definition:

  Objects are magnetic if they stick to a magnet at all.

- Periodically put objects back into the sand for more students to test.

- Remind students to try to keep sand in the sand table. Sweep up sand from the floor if necessary.

Activity 3: Sifting Sand and Beans

Overview

In this activity, students visit the sand learning station and find that things have changed. The objects they tested with magnets have been replaced by beans and peas of various sizes. The new challenge is to use a variety of sifters to separate the sand from the beans, and to separate one type of bean from the others.

Concepts explored include the idea that objects can be described by the property of size, and that tools can be helpful in filtering and separating mixtures. Through their experiences at the learning station, students become more aware of the connection between the size of an object and the hole it is able to go through. Once again, the idea of repeatability of results is reinforced. During the concluding discussion and demonstration, they see that something with *very* tiny holes (paper towel) is necessary to separate a sand/water mixture.

The ways students use sifters and filters in this activity makes an important connection to larger ideas in science, technology, and design. For information on the universality of sifting in science, please see "Behind the Scenes" on page 65.

Sifters and filters may be a familiar part of children's lives, from tea bags and coffee filters to colanders and sand toys. Once again, however, it is important to provide plenty of time for free exploration at the sifting learning station, and to allow students to learn more about the "nature of science" by **doing** science! Among the skills developed in this activity are: observing, predicting, comparing, testing, sorting, classifying, and communicating.

What You Need

For the class:
- ❏ 1 two-liter clear, colorless plastic soda bottle
- ❏ 1 pair of sharp scissors to cut the two-liter soda bottle
- ❏ 2 clear cups (each about 1 cup volume)
- ❏ several paper towels (coffee filters, about 10" in diameter, flat or cone-shaped may be substituted) for the class demonstration
- ❏ 1 paper towel for each pair of students
- ❏ broom and dust pan

For the learning station:
- ❏ 1 restaurant bus tub **OR** 2 standard dish tubs **OR** a sand table from Activity 2
- ❏ sand (enough to fill the tubs to about 4")
- ❏ at least 5 colanders/sifters/strainers with different-sized holes (for example, berry baskets with differing mesh, flour sifter, salad spinner basket, colander, various strainers). Find sifters first, and then choose beans. See "Getting Ready Before the Day of the Activity" for more information.
- ❏ at least 3 different-sized beans (lima beans, split peas, red kidney beans, etc.) See "Getting Ready Before the Day of the Activity" for more information on the sizes of beans you'll need.
- ❏ 4 plastic cups for scooping sand
- ❏ 4 box lids or cafeteria trays to catch sand as students sift
- ❏ 1 copy of the Activity Task Card for Volunteers (master on page 46)
- ❏ (*optional*) newspaper or a sheet to cover the sand table
- ❏ (*optional*) a tarp to go under the sand table
- ❏ (*optional*) tiny shiny confetti stars or other shapes

Note: The Full Option Science System (FOSS) module, Solids and Liquids, includes a kit with screens to use in sifting activities. See the "Resources" section, pages 58.

Some teachers suggest buying a package of 15-bean soup mix.

Getting Ready

Before the Day of the Activity

1. If possible, arrange for an adult to monitor the learning station. Give them an idea what to expect, and make them a copy of the Activity Task Card for Volunteers (master on page 46).

2. Sifters should have a variety of distinctly different-sized holes. Try to include one with very tiny holes that allows only sand through. Parents may be able to donate or loan some sifters. Flea markets, second-hand stores, and garage sales are other possible sources.

3. Once you have a selection of sifters, take time to "audition" your beans and peas. Try sifting a few yourself to make sure that there are at least some beans that can be separated successfully from the rest with the sifters available. You don't need to arrange it so that every bean is perfectly matched with a sifter, but most of your beans should be separable from the others and from the sand.

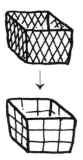

Sometimes strawberry baskets have holes so big that all the beans go through. To make the holes smaller, it is sometimes possible to nest two baskets with different-shaped holes.

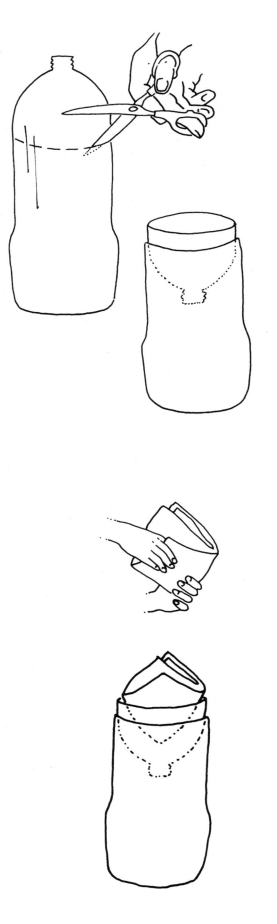

4. Make a funnel and container out of the two-liter bottle:

    a. Cut off the top part of the bottle at a point about 1" down from where the sides begin to curve.

    b. Turn the top piece upside down, and it becomes a funnel! Set the funnel part into the bottom part of the bottle which will serve as a large, clear container to catch the water after it drips through the funnel.

5. Make a paper towel into a cone-shaped filter (or substitute a coffee filter, about 10" in diameter, flat or cone-shaped):

    a. Fold a paper towel into four quarters.

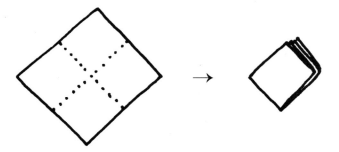

    b. Find the corner of the folded towel that has four separate edges, and grasp the towel by the *opposite* corner, which will become the bottom point of the cone.

    c. Pull one of the four separate corners away from the other three, creating a cone shape. (One side of the cone has three layers of thickness and the other side has one.)

    d. Set the filter cone into the funnel.

    e. To prepare for your class demonstration (page 44), you might want to practice pouring a small amount of sand and water through your filter. (If you do practice, make a new filter for the class demonstration.)

On the Day of the Activity

1. Set up the learning station: Mix the beans (and shiny confetti if you choose to use it) into the sand. Add the sifters and four plastic cups for scooping. Set the box lids or trays near the sand tub.

2. Set up your introduction area: Borrow three sifters with varying sized holes from the learning station. Also borrow a mixture of sand and beans in a clear cup.

3. For the day when you'll wrap up Activity 3, plan to have the following in the discussion area: all the sifters, a few samples of the different kinds of beans, a stack of paper towels, a cup half-filled with water, a cup half-filled with sand, the filter system made from the two-liter bottle including the paper towel filter.

Introducing Sifting

1. Have students sit in a circle, and tell them that today they'll have a different challenge at a new learning station. Hold up the cup of sand mixed with beans, and tell them that you were planning to make some pretend bean soup, but found out that all of the beans were mixed up with sand! Ask, "How could we separate the beans from the sand?" Let them know that you have some tools that might make it easier than using their hands.

2. Show the three sifters and ask, "What is the **same** about these three sifters?" [they have holes] "What is different about them?" [size, shape, hole size, etc.] For younger students you may want to demonstrate how to use one of the sifters.

3. Resist the temptation to give the students more instruction during your introduction, so they can explore for themselves. Tell them that the sand at the learning station is full of beans. Their challenge as sifting scientists is to use the sifters to separate the beans from the sand, and to separate different kinds of beans from each other.

4. Explain that it is important for them to sift carefully and gently, so sand doesn't get in anyone's eyes or on the floor. Return the "borrowed items" to the learning station.

Monitoring the Learning Station

1. Allow students plenty of time to freely explore at the learning station. Make sure everyone has at least one chance to visit the station.

2. If another adult will be assisting, explain the open-ended, discovery nature of the activity, and give them a copy of the Activity Task Card for Volunteers. You or whoever monitors the station should:

- Periodically put beans back into the sand.

- Remind students to sift over the sand tub or over one of the trays or box lids.

- Sweep sand off the floor.

- Encourage students to try all sifters.

- Ask questions such as, "Which sifter works best for you?" "Why?" "What's your favorite sifter?" "Why?"

- Challenge the students to use the sifters to separate one kind of bean from the mixture of sand and beans. (If a student uses fingers to pick out the beans, say that is one way that works, but suggest that they try to use a sifter to do the same thing.)

- If appropriate, encourage students to discover a method for separating each type of bean. They might find they need to sift several times, using sifters with holes of different sizes.

Discussing the Learning Station

1. Gather all sifters, a few samples of the different kinds of beans, a stack of paper towels, a cup half-filled with water, a cup half-filled with sand, the filter system made from the two-liter bottle, and the paper towel filter.

2. After students have all had time at the learning station, gather them in the discussion area. Hold up the sifter with the tiniest holes. Ask, "Was anything able to go through this sifter?" [sand] Ask the students to raise their hand if they were able to make a pile of just sand.

3. Choose one type of bean, and ask, "How did you get this kind of bean away from the others?" Ask students to explain why a specific sifter worked, encouraging them to discuss the size of the holes.

4. Repeat the question with one or two other types of beans, asking students to explain ways to separate them from all the rest. If students found methods of sifting with more than one sifter in sequence, help them explain their method by asking for each step in their process.

5. You may want to ask students if they found anything that wouldn't go through the sifter with the largest holes? Did they find anything that would go through the sifter with the tiniest holes? Can they think of anything else not on the table that might go through the sifter with the tiniest holes? [Some students may say "air" or "water" which leads into the next part of the activity.]

Separating Sand from Water

1. Pour the water into the half-filled cup of sand. Ask if any of the sifters could be used to separate this mixture of sand and water.

2. Ask students to predict what will happen when you pour the sand/water mixture through the sifter with the biggest holes.

3. Go ahead and pour the mixture through the sifter, catching what goes through in the empty cup that once held the water. *Note*: Sometimes the sand sticks to the top cup as you pour, and needs to be scooped out a bit.

4. Now ask the students to predict what will happen when you pour the mixture through the sifter with the smallest

There are usually many possible strategies for separating a mixture. For example:

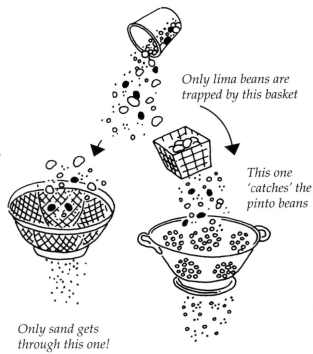

Only lima beans are trapped by this basket

This one 'catches' the pinto beans

Only sand gets through this one!

Sand and peas still need separating here

Perhaps the sifter has holes that are small enough to catch all the beans except the smallest ones, or holes big enough to let through all but the biggest kind of bean.

5. Help students draw the conclusion that the holes in all the sifters are too big, so they allow both the sand and the water to pass through.

Using a Paper Towel

1. Ask them what is needed to separate this mixture. [something with **tiny** holes] Pass out a paper towel to each pair of students. Have them hold the towel up to the light and look through it to see the holes.

2. Ask them to predict what will happen if you pour the mixture through the paper towel being used as a sifter or filter.

3. Take your paper towel filter out of the funnel, unfold it and show it to the class. Refold the paper towel, and set it into the funnel as before.

4. Pour the sand/water mixture into the filter and watch with the students as the water drains through the towel, leaving the sand caught in the towel. Ask the students to report what happened.

5. Review that a sifter with tiny holes is necessary to separate something tiny like sand from water.

6. If possible, have students return to the learning station to pursue some of the following challenges.

You could also have them pass one or several paper towels around. This may take longer, but will save paper towels. Or, if students will be going back to the learning station, you could have these extra paper towels available at the station so students can try using them as filters (see "Going Further" #1, page 45).

If some of your students are not familiar with "filters" you could briefly say what they are and explain that they are a special type of sifter.

Going Further

1. Have students use the extra paper towels to filter out some sand from water. Provide opportunities for students to filter other mixtures that contain water, such as water and soil.

2. Have older students write in their journals about the sifters they used and show which bean was separated using which sifter. They could also illustrate their writing. Younger students could draw one or more of the sifters they used.

3. Encourage students to bring in different sifters and explain what they are used for by the family at home. Teacher and students can also bring in different-sized beans, grains, and other objects to separate. These new sifters could also be written about and/or illustrated in journals.

4. Challenge students to create their own sifters out of meat trays, paper cups, paper plates, etc. for specific purposes. For instance, can they make a sifter that does not allow rice or peppercorns to go through it?

5. Consider cooking real bean soup or chili in a crock pot in the classroom!

6. Try putting salt, rice, and popcorn in a jar. Shake from side to side. Do the smaller items tend toward the bottom? Are layers formed? This suggests another method of separating materials.

7. For an art project, have students use rice, beans, and peas to create pictures.

Sifting Sand and Beans

Activity Task Card for Volunteers

Your goal is to assist the students in making their own discoveries, while keeping the activity safe, and the mess under control. As needed, remind students of the challenge, but refrain from demonstrating how it is done. Here's what the students are to do:

- Encourage students to try all sifters and to explore freely.

- Challenge the students to separate one kind of bean. If a student uses fingers to pick out the beans, say that is one way that works, but suggest that they try to use a sifter to do the same thing.

- If appropriate, encourage students to discover a method for separating each type of bean. They might find they need to sift several times, using sifters with holes of different sizes.

- Ask questions such as, "Which sifter works best for you?" "Why?" "What's your favorite sifter?" "Why?"

As they experiment with different sifters, ask open-ended questions, such as:

- What have you discovered?
- What's happening? Is that what you thought would happen?
- Did any of the sifters do something different than what you guessed?
- What surprised you?

If students get involved in explorations unrelated to separating the beans, you might want to steer them gently back on task. Make sure to intervene if you see an unsafe behavior. However, keep in mind that what may appear as "fooling around" can lead to some of the deepest learning experiences. Some of the greatest scientific discoveries have been made when scientists freely and creatively explored and imagined!

Young students need ample time to explore and work with the materials before tackling more structured challenges. Resist the temptation to give explanations to students. Your main role is to keep the station stocked and ready for more students to freely explore it.

Tips for Managing the Station

- Remind students to sift over the sand tub or one of the trays or box lids.

- Periodically put beans back into the tub for more students to sift.

- Sweep sand off the floor.

Activity 4: Garbage Dumps

Overview

In contrast to the learning station format used previously, this is an activity for the whole class, with students working in groups of four. The activity ties together what students have discovered about properties of various objects at the learning stations. It's an involving and culminating challenge to the entire unit, and serves as an excellent assessment of student learning at the stations.

Each student receives a make-believe "garbage dump:" a cup containing salt, sand, metal, and wax. The challenge is to separate the mixture without touching it with their hands. They draw upon their earlier experiences, using water to make the wax float out, a magnet to remove the metal, and a sifter with tiny holes to separate the water from the sand. And what can be done with separated garbage? It can be recycled! This lesson provides a perfect springboard for recycling activities or other related environmental school projects.

After completing the separations, the students are faced with the question, "What happened to the salt?" The teacher collects the water and pours it over a tray lined with black construction paper. Over time, the students observe the tray, looking for changes. Eventually, the water evaporates, leaving beautiful salt crystals attached to the black paper. Yes, the salt was in the water all along.

Skills developed include: cooperation, using suitable tools to address a specific task, and using previous experiences in new situations. Among the concepts explored are: mixtures and separating mixtures, dissolving, filtering, and evaporation. Students learn that many materials can be recycled and used again, sometimes in different forms.

As the activity is written, the teacher guides the whole class through each step in separating the "garbage dumps." Please feel free to adapt the teaching format to your students. Teachers of prekindergarten students may want to break this activity into several sessions, and some may choose to omit the salt from the activity. Teachers of older students may decide to present the activity in a less teacher-directed way, minimizing the times they stop for whole group instructions and discussion. Notes in the margin will alert you to more open-ended or teacher-directed options. For older students with lots of activity-based science experience, after the opening discussion, you could present the challenge and encourage them to proceed on their own.

What You Need

For the class:
- ❏ 1 waterproof tray with 1" high sides, at least 9" x 13"
- ❏ black construction paper to fit on the bottom of the tray
- ❏ 1 pair of sharp scissors to cut the two-liter soda bottles
- ❏ towels or newspaper in case of spills

For each group of four students:
- ❏ 4 magnets (or 2 per group if students are sharing)
- ❏ 4 clear plastic cups, 8–10 oz. each
- ❏ 4 wax birthday candles
- ❏ sand, about 4 tablespoons
- ❏ salt, about 4 teaspoons (kosher salt is preferable)
- ❏ 20 metal paper clips
- ❏ 4 plastic spoons
- ❏ 2 paper cups (small, 3 oz. size is fine)
- ❏ 1 water bottle or cup with pour spout, at least 16 oz. capacity
- ❏ 1 two-liter plastic soda bottle cut to make a funnel (clear plastic bottles are preferable but not required)
- ❏ 1 paper towel (a coffee filter, about 10" in diameter, flat or cone-shaped may be substituted)
- ❏ (*optional*) 1 cafeteria tray for equipment

See the "Resources" section, page 58, for curriculum materials to extend the study of recycling and reuse.

Getting Ready

Before the Day of the Activity

1. Using the directions in "Getting Ready Before the Day of the Activity" in Activity 3 (page 40), make additional two-liter bottle filter systems. You'll need a filter system for each group of four students.

2. Insert folded paper towels or filter papers into the funnels.

3. Read over the instructions for presenting this activity, and decide how much direction you want to provide for your students as they separate the "garbage" mixture in their cups. Teachers of younger students will probably want to lead the students through the activity together, in a step-by-step manner, as written in the guide. For older students, teachers may prefer to introduce the challenge, distribute all materials, and allow students to proceed independently in their small groups.

4. If possible, arrange for an adult helper to distribute materials as they are needed, and to collect distracting materials after they are used. Volunteers can also make and clean up the "garbage dumps."

On the Day of the Activity

1. Make a "garbage dump" for each student: add about one teaspoon of salt and about one tablespoon of sand to each plastic cup. Cut each candle into three pieces. Place three pieces of candle and five metal paper clips in each cup. Do not stir, so students will be able to tell what the ingredients are.

2. Arrange materials for each group of four students (on trays if you have them) with: four "garbage dumps," four spoons, and two paper cups. Keep materials ready for quick distribution after your introduction.

3. Set up additional materials to pass out to each table of four during the activity: magnets, one water bottle about half-full of water, and a filter system (including the paper towel filter).

4. For the concluding discussion, line one large tray with black construction paper for the whole class.

The Mini "Garbage Dump"

1. Ask students if they separate any garbage at home. Why? [for composting or recycling] Say that cities and towns have so much garbage, that we may run out of space at the dumps someday! Some of the garbage could be separated so it can be used again.

2. Say, "It would take a long time to separate garbage by hand, and it would be very messy besides. That's why scientists and workers have come up with some ways to separate garbage **without using their hands.**"

3. Show a mini "garbage dump" and say that it is made up of pretend garbage that's all mixed up.

4. Their job as "garbage separation scientists" will be to separate the different items in the "garbage dump." They will use what they learned at the learning stations, and some of the tools they used before.

If you have opted for a less directed activity format, you won't need the step-by-step directions outlined in Steps 2 through 6. Instead, introduce the challenge of separating the candles and paper clips, say what tools are available, and allow students to proceed independently in their groups. Then refocus the class before separating the sand. Be sure to encourage groups to help each other and share ideas.

The brief group discussion before the question is asked of the entire class in Step 2, and in other steps below, encourages all students to remember their learning station experiences and helps focus their responses when the same question is asked of the entire class. If you find it hard to keep shifting gears, you could consider not having the small group discussions or modifying the procedure to suit your own predilections and the needs of your students.

With younger students, it is best to model the procedure in Step 3 and assist in pouring the water.

5. Say that they can move the "garbage" around with their spoons, but they should not touch it with their hands. Encourage them to look carefully to figure out what is in the "garbage."

6. Pass out the "garbage dumps," spoons, and paper cups.

Separating the Wax and Metal

1. Regain the attention of the class, and ask them what they see in their pretend "garbage dumps." [sand, wax, metal paper clips, salt] Record all the materials on the board, making sure they know the white particles are salt.

2. Circle WAX on the board. Ask students, in their groups of four, to very briefly discuss what they learned about wax at the sink/float learning station and how they could separate the wax from the rest of the "garbage." Then ask the class, "How can we separate the wax from the rest of the 'garbage' without touching any of it?" Accept several answers without judging the responses. As needed, ask questions to remind students of the sink/float learning station activity. Ask what might happen to the wax candle if water was poured into the "garbage dump."

3. Instruct students that they will pour a small amount of water (about 1", which is about the length of a paper clip) into their cup until they see the wax floating. Next, they will use their spoons to remove the wax and put all pieces of wax from their "garbage dumps" into one of the paper cups.

4. Pass a water bottle to each table and tell the students to proceed. **As groups finish pouring, remove the water bottles from the tables.**

5. Refocus the class, and circle METAL on the board. Ask students, in their groups of four, to briefly discuss what they learned about metal at the magnet learning station and how they could separate the metal from the "garbage." Then ask the entire class, "What did we learn about metal?" Ask, "What tool can we use to separate metal from the rest of the 'garbage'?"

6. Instruct students that they will use magnets to separate and remove the metal paper clips. They will put all the paper clips from their "garbage dumps" into the other paper cup. Pass out the magnets, tell the students to proceed, and collect the magnets again as soon as students have finished.

7. Circle SAND on the board. Ask students, in their groups of four, to very briefly discuss what they learned about sand at the sifting learning station and how they could separate the sand from the "garbage." Then ask the entire class, "How can we separate the sand from the water?" [by using a sifter with *very* tiny holes] Explain that they will get a filter system and take turns pouring what is left in their "garbage dump" into it. They can use their spoon to scoop the sand into the filter if it gets stuck in the "garbage dump."

Separating the Sand

1. Tell students that when they finish, they should leave the filter system on their group's table, but bring their cups of paper clips and wax to the discussion area.

2. Pass one filter system to each group, and have them begin separating the sand from the water.

3. Collect the cups of wax and paper clips as student groups come to the discussion area.

Reflecting on the Activity

What Happened to the Salt?

1. In the discussion area, focus on the list of the "garbage" they have separated up to this point. Review how the wax,

It's okay if you can't fit all the water onto the tray. Pour a substantial amount of the salt water, so as many crystals as possible will form.

The Involving Dissolving *GEMS guide for Grades 1–3 (with adaptations for prekindergarten and Kindergarten) would be a natural unit to follow* Sifting Through Science, *for additional experiences with solids, liquids, and dissolving.*

paper clips, and sand were separated. Circle SALT on the board and ask, "Where is the salt?" [They might answer: in the sand, in the water, in the air, or it disappeared.]

2. Tell them that as a class, they'll do an experiment to see if the salt went into the water. Tell them that you will collect all the water they filtered and pour it onto the tray with the black construction paper.

3. Ask for any ideas about what might happen to the water if you leave the tray of water in a safe place for a while—maybe a day or three days or a week.

4. Explain that they have an important job—to observe the tray carefully over the next several days.

5. After the discussion, collect the water from their filter systems, pour it on the tray, and set it in a secure but accessible place. The water should evaporate, leaving beautiful salt crystals on the black paper. You can cut the paper in pieces for the students to take home.

Making the Connection to Recycling

1. Tell the class they have been great "garbage separation scientists." Ask them what can be done with the materials they've separated. Accept reasonable answers, including the re-use of these materials. [give paper clips to school secretary, use in art projects, etc.]

2. Ask students who recycle at home about the different groupings or sortings they make (newspaper, glass, aluminum). By doing this, they are starting the process of sorting the garbage. Point out that this is a good thing to do, because it means less is thrown away and more is recycled.

3. Ask if students have any questions about the activity or about recycling and the environment. How could the class find out more about community environmental resources?

4. If possible, provide some of the different "garbage dump" mixtures listed as "Going Further" on the next page. These could also serve as excellent assessment activities. Groups of students could create "garbage dumps" for other groups to separate.

Going Further

1. If possible, schedule more class sharing time. Encourage older students to write and draw in their journals or in a class book.

2. Create other "garbage dumps" for students to separate themselves. One example, Garbage Mystery #1, would be to mix pieces of plastic or styrofoam, different metal objects (BBs or washers), glass beads, and Epsom salts. The resulting crystals would be different than the ones formed in the main activity. Garbage Mystery #2 might be paper clips, pieces of aluminum foil, sugar, and pieces of wood. Or you could make other mystery "garbage dumps." Here are some more ideas to add to the mix:

---

something magnetic: paper clips, BBs, washers, bolts

something that floats: wax, pieces of wood, plastic, styrofoam

something that dissolves and makes crystals: salt, sugar, Epsom salts

something non-magnetic that doesn't float or dissolve: sand, glass beads, aluminum foil

---

3. Set up recycling bins in the classroom. If they don't already exist in the school lunchroom, encourage your class to take the lead in setting them up. Discuss recycling and reuse. Ask students to think about things in the classroom that could be reused or recycled.

4. Learn how to make paper, reusing discarded scraps from other projects. Use scraps of paper to make colorful collages.

5. Have students save their garbage from lunch one day and bring it back to class. Sort and classify it into recyclable or not-recyclable. Record how many of each there are. Then consider the question—how much non-recyclable material can be replaced by recyclable material? For example, instead of buying snacks in individual bags, snacks could be bought in bigger boxes and a small amount put in a reusable plastic container each school day. Or how about using a thermos instead of a juice box? Cloth sacks or lunch boxes can be used instead of brown bags. After one week, examine garbage from lunch again. This time how many items are recyclable and how many

are not? What about the lunches served in the cafeteria? How much is recyclable and how much is thrown away?

6. Visit a recycling center. Or have an educator or activist from a local environmental group who regularly discusses these topics with young children come in and talk about garbage, recycling, and related matters.

7. Set up worm boxes to learn more about how soil is recycled and how earthworms contribute to the environment. See the "Resources" section in this guide and consider presenting the GEMS guide *Terrarium Habitats*.

8. Have the class take part in Earth Day or other activities that educate the general population about recycling and the environment.

9. Consider, either as an assessment activity, or just for creative fun, having students design a robot that can separate garbage and assist in other environmentally friendly tasks. To start with, how would the robot separate the same materials as the class "garbage dumps?"

10. Encourage students to start or improve recycling at home and get parents involved too. You could also gather aluminum cans at school and home and cash them in to raise money for recycling bins or other environmental projects.

Resources

Sources for Materials

Vinyl Real Graph

> Teaching Resource Center
> P.O. Box 1509
> San Leandro, CA 94577
> phone: (800) 833-3389
> fax: (800) 972-7722

Magnets

> Safari Ltd.
> P.O. Box 630685
> Miami, FL 33163
> phone: (800) 615-3111 (information for regional representative)
> phone: (800) 858-2455 (CA order only)

> NASCO
> 4825 Stoddard Rd.
> Modesto, CA 95356-9318
> phone: (800) 558-9595

> These two sources carry fun, colorful magnets in a variety of shapes and sizes. Most hardware stores will carry plain black (but very functional) magnets.

Related Curriculum

The Full Option Science System (FOSS), developed at the Lawrence Hall of Science, includes a number of modules that relate to the activities in *Sifting Through Science*.

> The FOSS Wood Module, for Kindergarten, calls for students to compare the properties of different kinds of wood, and includes an investigation of wood in water and what it takes to sink samples of wood.

> The Solids and Liquids Module, as well as the Pebbles, Sand, and Silt Module, both for Grades 1 and 2, also include activities that complement

this unit. Students investigate particulate solids (corn meal, beans, rice) and liquids (water, corn syrup, oil) and compare their behavior and interactions. In Pebbles, Sand, and Silt, students sort, wash, compare, and seriate rocks. They also separate mixtures of rocks with screens, and investigate clay and soil.

The FOSS K–6 program also includes a module on Magnetism and Electricity. Although designed for Grades 3 and 4, you may want to adapt some of its explorations of permanent and electromagnetism if you and your students are eager to delve further into this fascinating and powerful phenomenon.

Study of sand is featured in several GEMS guides, including *Terrarium Habitats,* for Grades K–6, and *On Sandy Shores,* for Grades 2–4.

General Resources

100 Best Ideas for Primary Science, Beverly Hartman, Teaching & Learning Company, Carthage, Illinois, 1994.

> A book of hands-on activities intended to build a firm foundation of scientific skills and thinking processes. Includes float/sink and magnet activities.

How Is A Crayon Made?, Oz Charles, Simon & Schuster, New York, 1988.

> Describes, in text and step-by-step photographs, the manufacture of a crayon from wax to finished product.

Mudpies to Magnets: A Preschool Science Curriculum, Robert A. Williams, Robert E. Rockwell, Elizabeth A. Sherwood, Gryphon House, Beltsville, Maryland, 1987.

> A collection of hands-on learning activities for preschoolers arranged by grade level and curriculum units.

Sandbox Scientist: Real Science Activities for Little Kids, Michael E. Ross, Chicago Review Press, Chicago, 1995.

> A guide for adults in setting up activities for children ages two to eight to experience scientific principles

about water, matter, air, light, etc., using familiar materials. A wonderful source of open-ended lessons for young children.

Sift and Shout: Sand Play Activities For 1-6 Year Olds, Randy F. Granovetter and Jeanne C. James, Kaplan Press, Lewisville, North Carolina, 1989.

A handbook of activities which integrate cognitive, fine motor, and gross motor skills; reinforce scientific ideas and mathematical concepts. Activities are organized by age group, and can be conducted in dishpans, sand tables, sandboxes, or at the beach. Craft activities included.

What Are Scientists?, Rita Golden Gelman and Susan Kovacs Buxbaum, Scholastic, New York, 1991.

Introduces scientists—beyond their stereotypes—as regular people, then describes many types of scientists, their work, and the places they study. The importance of scientific inquiry is stressed and a real-world connection to scientists is made.

Sink/Float Resources

Boats that Float, Rita Golden Gelman and Susan Kovacs Buxbaum, Watts, New York, 1981.

Since this GEMS guide was first published, several additional resource books have been recommended, including: Making Things Float and Sink *and* Playing with Magnets, *both published by Copper Beech Books, an imprint of The Millbrook Press; and* Keep It Afloat *by Julian Rowe and Molly Perham, Children's Press, Chicago, 1993.*

Instructions for making 11 different boats from common items. When finished, each boat will float.

Science Fun with Toy Boats and Planes, Rose Wyler, Julian Messner, New York, 1986.

Easy experiments to do at home or school with home equipment, showing basic principles of how boats float and move and how planes fly.

Water and Floating, David Evans and Claudette Williams, Dorling Kindersley, New York, 1993.

A great book for extending students' explorations of water. Contains activities that use simple observations and experiments to explore the properties of water.

Magnetism Resources

All About Magnets, Stephen Krensky, Scholastic, New York, 1993.

Amazing Magnets, Julian Rowe and Molly Perham, Children's Press, Danbury, Connecticut, 1994.

Batteries, Bulbs, and Wires, David Glover, Kingfisher Books, New York, 1993.

> Uses activities and projects to introduce how electricity and magnets work at home and in the everyday world.

Electricity and Magnets, Terry Cash, Warwick Press, New York, 1989.

> Describes the discovery of electricity, how it is generated, and the links between electricity and magnetism. Includes instructions for experiments and games using magnets.

Experiments with Magnets, Helen J. Challand, Childrens Press, Chicago, 1986.

> Suggests experiments introducing magnets and magnetism, demonstrating the magnetic field and the properties, strength, and uses of magnets.

Exploring Magnetism, Neil Ardley, F. Watts, New York, 1983.

> Explains the basic principles of magnetism and suggests a variety of experiments which use magnets.

My First Batteries & Magnets Book, Jack Challoner, Dorling Kindersley, New York, 1992.

> Experiments and activities introduce the properties of batteries and magnets and the principles of electricity and magnetism.

My Magnet, Robert Pressling, Gareth Stevens, Milwaukee, Wisconsin, 1994.

The Mystery of Magnets, Melvin Berger, Newbridge Communications, New York, 1995.

Science Book of Magnets, Neil Ardley, Harcourt Brace Jovanovich, San Diego, 1991.

Contains clear color photos and easy to follow directions. Depicts activities using bar magnets, horseshoe magnets, and electric magnets. Sidebars relate how magnetic principles are used in science and industry.

What Magnets Can Do, Allan Fowler, Children's Press, Danbury, Connecticut, 1995.

Recyling Resources

Buried in Garbage, Bobbie Kalman and Janine Schaub, Crabtree Publishing, Ontario, Canada, 1991.

Describes what garbage is, why it has become a problem, and what happens to it at the landfill or incineration site. Text, photos, and diagrams show how garbage is separated. Also includes information on recycling and composting.

Cartons, Cans, and Orange Peels: Where Does Your Garbage Go?, Joanna Foster, Clarion Books, New York, 1991.

Outlines the composition of garbage and trash and discusses the various methods of disposing of it with an emphasis on recycling.

Compost! A Teacher's Guide to Activities & Resources in the East Bay, Cindy Nelson, Sarah Shaffer, and Cindy Havstad, Alameda County Home Composting Program, 7977 Capwell Dr., Oakland, CA 94621, (510) 635-6275.

This is an excellent series of activities on composting and recycling, with well-summarized information and an excellent listing of related resources.

Compost! Growing Gardens From Your Garbage, Linda Glaser, The Millbrook Press, Brookfield, Connecticut, 1996.

Aimed at the very young child, this picture book describes what composting is, what it does, and how to go about it.

Composting Across the Curriculum: A Teacher's Guide to Composting, Marin County Office of Waste Management, 3501 Civic Center Dr., Room 403, San Rafael, CA 94903-4177, (415) 499-6647.

An outstanding collection of activities for preschool through adult. This guide contains 26 clearly written lessons plus instruction on how to compost, vocabulary, background information for teachers and designs for building your own compost or worm bin.

The Compost Heap, Harlow Rockwell, Doubleday, New York, 1974.

Dinosaurs to the Rescue! A Guide to Protecting Our Planet, Laurie Krasny Brown and Marc Brown, Little, Brown, Boston, 1992.

Text and illustrations of dinosaur characters introduce the earth's major environmental problems and suggest ways children can help.

Fast Plants/Bottle Biology, University of Wisconsin, Department of Plant Pathology, 1630 Linden Dr., Madison, WI 53706, (608) 263-5645.

Contains hundreds of great activities you can do with two-liter bottles.

From Food to Fertilizer, Charles C. Dahlberg, Young Scott Books, New York, 1973.

Diagrams the food chain for young readers.

It Zwibble: Earthday Birthday, Italtoons Corp., Family Home Entertainment, Van Nuys, California, 1991.

Videocasette for ages 3 and up. The Zwibble Dibble dinosaurs—funny, friendly creatures dedicated to protecting the Earth—throw a birthday bash for planet Earth to remind people how important the environment is.

Let's Talk Trash: The Kid's Book About Recycling, Kelly McQueen and David Fassler, M.D., with the Environmental Law Foundation, Waterfront Books, 1991.

Recycle! A Handbook for Kids, Gail Gibbons, Little, Brown, Boston, 1992.

Explains the process of recycling from start to finish and discusses what happens to paper, glass, aluminum cans, and plastic when they are recycled into new products.

The Rotten Truth, Children's Television Workshop, 3-2-1 Contact Series, Pleasantville, New York, 1990.

Videocasette plus teacher's guide. Learn the "rotten truth" about garbage. Come along with Stepanie Yu as she visits a landfill, leads a tour through the Museum of Modern Garbage, and much more. Most appropriate for older students.

Waste Education Clearinghouse Listing of Materials Available, Waste Education Clearinghouse, OWM, 1350 Energy Lane, St. Paul, MN 55108, (800) 677-6300.

A catalog of free waste education materials.

Worms Eat My Garbage, Mary Appelhof, Flower Press, Kalamazoo, Michigan, 1982.

A complete and practical guide to worm composting.

Behind the Scenes

The following information is provided for your information as the teacher. It is not meant to be read out loud to or duplicated for students. A word of caution: topics such as the universality of "sifting" in science, magnetism, and buoyancy are best understood at much higher grade levels. We hope the background we provide will be helpful to you in providing a general context for building the foundation for these concepts and for student questions that may arise. In later grades students will have the opportunity to find out more about sinking and floating, investigate magnetism in greater depth, and use sophisticated laboratory techniques derived from the basic ideas about separation they experience in this unit. The emphasis in this guide is on free exploration and on students constructing intuitive understandings of these important concepts.

The information on garbage disposal, separation, and recycling is summarized from several sources. Books in the "Resources" section provide excellent and accessible information and illustrations for younger students on these subjects.

On Floating and Sinking

Whether an object sinks or floats is a fairly simple question to explore directly, as your students do in this unit. To explain it, on the other hand, requires a grasp of a number of physical science concepts, as well as mathematical applications. Among these concepts are mass, weight, density, volume, surface tension, buoyancy, fluid pressure, and displacement.

The ancient Greek mathematician and inventor Archimedes studied buoyancy. He stated that any object completely or partially submerged in a fluid (liquid or gas) at rest is acted upon by an upward, or buoyant, force that is equal to the weight of the fluid that is displaced by the object. If the weight of an object is less than that of the displaced fluid, the object rises, as in the case of a block of wood released below the surface of the water. A ship that is launched sinks into the ocean until the weight of the water it displaces is equal to its own weight—as the ship is loaded it sinks deeper, displacing more water. The amount of buoyant force pushing it upward always matches the weight of the ship and its load. This force is also called upthrust. If the upthrust produced is equal to the weight of the boat, then it will float. Huge metal boats have to displace a large amount of water—this is why they are hollow and broad in shape.

Another famous scientist, Galileo, wrote a "Discourse on Things That Float" in which he worked out the conditions for the flotation of solid bodies in a liquid. Early hands-on experiences will spark the interest of your students and help prepare them for later, more formal study. Students who keep journals could write their own "Discourse on Things That Float!"

The Force of Magnetism

Magnetism is a force that is a property of matter (and of the Earth itself). It is one form of electromagnetic energy, which includes electricity, magnetism, light, and heat.

Only two materials found in nature, lodestone (also called magnetite, an oxide of iron, Fe_3O_4 found in igneous rocks) and another iron compound, pyrrhotite, are strongly magnetic, also called natural ferromagnets. In addition to these iron compounds, cobalt, nickel, and some alloys that combine iron, cobalt, or nickel have ferromagnetic capacity, as do a few rare earth elements. This means they magnetize easily and retain strong magnetic power (unless subjected to very high temperatures). These materials exhibit strong magnetic properties due to the motion and alignment of their electrons around the nucleus of their atoms. These atoms have permanent "magnetic moments," meaning they align in such a way as to be in and of themselves basic electromagnets. The atomic alignment of ferromagnetic substances as well as the susceptibility of other substances to magnetism are quite well understood (and far beyond the scope of this guide).

The magnetic properties of lodestone were known to ancient peoples. It is said that Greek shepherds sometimes noticed bits of lodestone sticking to the iron tips of their staffs. It is thought that the Chinese devised a magnetic compass as early as the 26th century B.C. William Gilbert, physician to Queen Elizabeth I, observed that the Earth is in fact a huge magnet. English physicist Joseph Priestley and French physicist Charles-Augustin de Coulomb experimentally investigated the forces between the poles of magnets.

In 1820 a Danish physicist, Hans Christian Ørsted, confirmed the long-suspected link between magnetism and electricity when he showed that an electric current flowing in a wire produces its own magnetic field. Ørsted's discovery was made while he was lecturing to a class of university students. By chance, he placed a wire carrying electric current near a compass needle and was surprised to see the needle swing at right angles to the wire.

Scientists wondered if the reverse was also true—whether a magnet could induce electricity. After 10 years of experiments, Michael Faraday proved that it could by building the first electric generator. He demonstrated that a magnet passing through a coil of wire induced a flow of electricity in the wire. Soon, these discoveries led to the development of the electromagnet and to more sophisticated generators and motors (which convert electric energy to mechanical energy). The discovery of the link between magnetism and electricity has been a major factor in industrialization, transportation, communications, and much of the technology of today's world.

Your students may ask which metals are attracted by magnets and which are not. Probably the best response is to emphasize that the explorations at the learning station can help them figure out that question for themselves. Objects that have iron, cobalt, or nickel in them should be attracted to a magnet. Probably most—if not all—of the items your students decide "stick" to the magnets will contain iron. Nickel-cadmium batteries are one common item that contain nickel.

On Sifting in Science

There are a vast number of techniques that scientists utilize to sift and separate materials. These separation techniques can be based on a large variety of physical properties and laboratory approaches. Separation of different particles from each other is an important process in both industry and research. These are usually done to: (1) remove particles from gases or liquids, or (2) separate particles of different sizes or properties.

Scientists separate mixtures for many reasons, including for purification purposes. A mixture may contain some substance or substances that should be isolated from the rest of the mixture: purification is the process of isolating and thus removing substances considered to be contaminants. For example, in the manufacture of synthetic drugs, mixtures with differing proportions of compounds result. The removal of any impurities as well as arrival at the desired and exact proportion of ingredients is important if the product is to have uniform strength and be free of other ingredients that might be dangerous to the body.

Among the most important particle separation methods are filtration (screening), sedimentation, elutriation, centrifugation, particle electrophoresis, electrostatic precipitation, foam fractionation, and flotation. There are numerous additional variations. The method that most closely reflects the work your students do in this unit is filtration or screening.

In filtration, a porous material is used to separate particles of different sizes. The same basic principles your students learn in the sifting activities apply. If the pore sizes are highly uniform, separation can be fairly sensitive to the size of the particles. This method is most commonly used to separate liquids from suspended crystals or other solids. To speed up filtration, pressure is often applied.

Here is one interesting filtration method: A series of sieves is stacked, with the screen with the largest hole size at the top. The mixture of particles is placed at the top, and the assembly is agitated to facilitate the passage of the particles through successive screens. At the end of the operation, the particles are distributed among the sieves according to their diameters. In a similar way, many laboratory methods depend on penetration of molecules through semi-permeable membranes. Some mixtures of materials can be separated based on the different **rates** at which they move through the same medium or through a semi-permeable membrane.

Garbage

It is estimated that an average family in the United States "produces" between 45 and 100 pounds of garbage **every week.** Of this, about one third is food and garden waste, including vegetable peels, fruit skins and cores, leftovers, garden clippings, and leaves. Nearly a quarter of the food we buy ends up being thrown out!

Another third of garbage is made up of paper or paper products, including empty boxes, packaging material, newspapers, mail, etc. The final third of garbage includes items made of glass, plastic, and metal, including many containers, such as jars, cans, and bottles. The pie chart, modified and adapted from the book *Buried in Garbage* and other sources (see "Resources" section), summarizes the proportions.

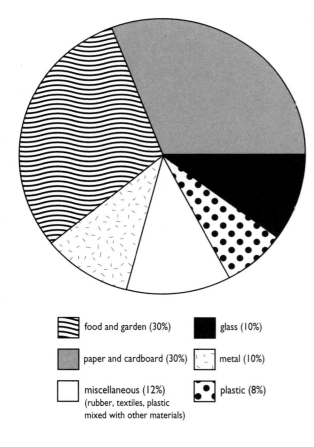

food and garden (30%)

paper and cardboard (30%)

miscellaneous (12%)
(rubber, textiles, plastic
mixed with other materials)

glass (10%)

metal (10%)

plastic (8%)

When garbage is collected in most cities it is taken to transfer stations, where some basic sorting may be done, and where it is compacted. It is then placed on large vehicles called transfer trailers and taken to either a landfill site or an incinerator. Many cities use a landfill system, which, while superior to open-air dumps, also has its drawbacks. Landfills use a layer of clay in an old gravel pit or valley to create a protective liner about five feet thick on the bottom and sides, and at the end of each day the waste is covered with soil to reduce odors and animal visits. This makes for alternating layers of dirt and garbage. When a landfill site is full, another thick layer of clay and more soil is placed on top.

Decomposition of landfill garbage leads to the release of gases, such as methane, that need to be vented to prevent fires and explosions. As garbage decomposes and rain mixes in, a poisonous liquid called leachate is produced and can seep into the ground. Although the clay liner prevents most of the leachate from seeping into the soil, leachate needs to be collected regularly and taken to a toxic waste facility or it can poison the ground water. Landfill sites need to be checked for many years after the site is no longer being used and the soil tested for contamination, as leachate continues to form.

For all their potential problems, landfill sites have served as a temporary and partial solution. But many urban landfills are full and there is little space available for more.

Many areas that now lack landfill space build incineration plants for solid waste. Prior to incineration, the garbage is sorted and separated. A conveyer belt takes the garbage from the unloading pit to a shredder. Slow turning shears rip open the bags and chop up the garbage. The garbage then moves through a magnetic separator. Metal is separated out from the rest of the garbage and compressed into cubes for recycling. It can be sold to industry. This is an interesting real-world parallel to what your students do in this unit.

The Three "Rs" and More

Many students, and a large proportion of the general populace, are aware of the serious issues posed by the buildup of garbage, as well as other related pollution and environmental concerns. From early consciousness-raising efforts some decades ago ("don't be a litterbug") to many modern recycling facilities, community programs, and educational outreach efforts, the increase in awareness and action has been striking.

Along with the well-known symbol for recycling, has come an oft-repeated three-word slogan to help people remember the basic concepts. These are the three "Rs," namely, reduce, recycle, and reuse. **Reduce** means to cut down on the amount of garbage that is generated. While this can mean reducing the amount of non-essential goods we buy, it can also include the idea of "precycling," which means deliberately purchasing products that already utilize recyclable materials, such as eggs in cardboard cartons rather than styrofoam or soft drinks in refillable bottles. Since packaging is such a large proportion of garbage, items that recycle their packaging (or are sold unwrapped) help reduce the amount of garbage.

Reuse has to do with saving items that would otherwise be thrown out and finding ways to use them again. Countless teachers utilize newspaper, paper scraps, yogurt containers, and many other items as manipulatives or containers or for art projects. **Recycling** means finding ways to turn some of what is discarded into new products. For example, making park benches or playground equipment from recycled plastic milk jugs. Although most community programs are called "recycling" programs, in fact putting cans, bottles, and newspapers into separate containers (technically called source separation) is only the first step toward recycling.

There are many excellent books and resources on recycling and the environment to assist you and your students to gain a fuller understanding of these issues. Since this unit is about separating materials from one another, you may want to encourage your students to learn more about composting. This is a very direct way of reducing the amount of garbage as well as a recognition of nature's recycling process. Composting involves separating food and other organic and/or biodegradable materials from other household garbage and allowing it to decompose naturally. Over time, it decomposes into humus, which is an excellent fertilizer, providing essential nutrients to the soil. Composting reduces the amount of garbage the household sends out, reuses the biodegradable materials to make humus, and recycles the garbage/humus as fertilizer to grow new fruits and vegetables. In addition to admirably fulfilling all three "Rs," composting also lessens the use of chemical fertilizers.

Special Note on Graphing

As your students experience in this unit, graphs can be very useful tools for organizing data. This section is designed to assist you in helping your students progress in their comprehension of and ability to create and use graphs.

To begin with, young students need concrete experiences creating and interpreting data with simple, meaningful graphs. For young students, graphing develops naturally from sorting and classifying activities and from their interest in comparing objects. Graphs become a tool to organize the sort or comparison. Once a graph is made, students can make "true statements" regarding, for example, quantities of distinct items on the graph, and make comparison statements that build on their understanding of "more" and "less."

When students make and interpret graphs, their work concerns many areas of mathematics, including statistics, measurement, and number. They also develop many skills, such as counting, comparing, problem-solving, and logical thinking, as well as organizing, visualizing, interpreting data, and drawing conclusions.

The GEMS Teacher's Guides Eggs, Eggs Everywhere *and* Treasure Boxes *also contain activities that provide students with interesting graphing experiences.*

Types of Graph

Real-object graphs, sometimes called real or concrete graphs, provide the foundation for all graphing activities at the primary level. The real-object graphs in the sink/float and the magnet activities are good examples. Real-object graphs compare concrete or real objects. Students have actually conducted hands-on, scientific explorations with these same objects and then use the graphs to organize their findings.

Pictorial graphs use pictures or models to represent the real objects. This type of graph is more abstract than a real-object graph, because any drawing of an object—even when drawn by the child—is more abstract than the object itself. The picture of the crayon that floated is *not* the crayon itself! Pictorial graphs provide an important link between real-object and more abstract (or symbolic) graphs, and they help prepare students for symbolic graphs. Making a pictorial graph is suggested for older students in both the sink/float and the magnet activities.

You can post the pictorial graph with questions that invite those viewing it to look closely at the data and try to make some sense of it.

Symbolic graphs are more abstract—they use symbols to represent the real objects. An "X" on piece of paper stands for an object that floated or was magnetic. To interpret these graphs, there must be an awareness of what the symbols represent. After plenty of experience with real-object and pictorial graphs, students are ready to move on to this type of graphing. Some second grade students may be able to record the sink/float, magnetic, or other data in this more abstract way.

Questioning Strategies and Data Interpretation

Once a graph is made, it provides a context for analyzing and interpreting the compiled data. It is important to assist student by asking questions. As the graph is created, you may want to stop along the way and ask questions about the data. It helps the students stay focused and gives them an opportunity to see how the graph changes as more data is added. By asking questions you can help foster their analytical skills and their statistical understanding. Here are some sample questions for a sink/float graph:

- How many objects floated?
- How many objects sank?
- Are there more _____ or more _____?
- Are there fewer _____ or fewer _____?
- Did more sink or float?
- How many more sank (floated)?
- Which has the most?
- Which has the fewest?
- How many fewer _____ than _____?
- How many objects are there are on the graph altogether?

When your students have had many experiences with graphing, more open-ended questions will allow you to access what your students have learned about interpreting data. Here are some examples of more open-ended questions:

- What can you tell me about this graph?
- Who can make a true statement about this graph?
- What does this graph compare?
- What does this graph tell us?

These questions lead to true statements or facts about the data. They help students analyze the data. The next step is interpretation of the data. What can we infer from this data? In the case of the graph about magnetic and non-magnetic objects, as students look at all the objects that are magnetic they can begin to look for attributes that make objects magnetic and make some generalizations. In doing so, they are making inferences based on their analysis of data from the graph.

Sequence of Learning

A sequence of graphing experiences that begins with real-object graphs and progresses to pictorial and then symbolic graphs will lead students from the concrete to the abstract. Along the way, there are incremental changes in each stage of graphing that help students take steps forward. The following is one sequence that promotes student learning of graphing concepts:

- Real-object Graphs   Comparing 2 and 3 groups   PreK–2

- Pictorial Graphs   Comparing 2 and 3 groups   K–2

- Real-object Graphs   Comparing 4 and more groups   K–2

- Pictorial Graphs   Comparing 4 groups   K–2

- Symbolic Graphs   Comparing 2 groups   1–2
    Comparing 3 groups   1–2 and above
    Comparing 4 and more groups   1–2 and above

Students work on real-object graphs that compare two and three groups over several grades, but these graphs can be varied to maintain student interest and provide new learning experiences. To do so, use a wide assortment of materials and vary the method of organizing the data. For example, students can graph things in the classroom (blocks, buttons, snack preferences, etc.) as well as things from home (play animals, an art tool, a ball, etc.). The graphs you make with this data can be displayed horizontally or vertically and, in some cases, real objects can be placed within a picture. For example, toy vehicles can be graphed by type and placed inside a picture of a corresponding vehicle, as illustrated below:

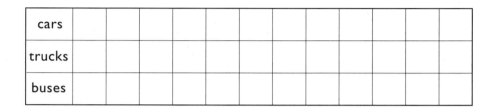

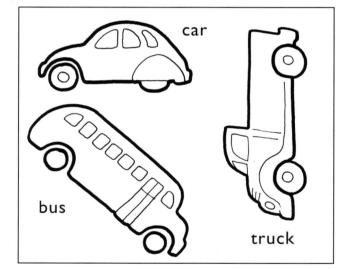

Large outlines of vehicles were drawn on butcher paper. Students "drove" their vehicles onto the appropriate one.

You are the best judge of the skills and abilities of your students. Allow them to progress at an appropriate pace; their progress can help determine the selection of the graphs that they create and analyze. When your students are ready, consider taking the same data through a sequence of all three types of graph. Students can then see the same data organized in three different ways and learn how the interpretation of the data should lead to similar conclusions. For example, make a real-object graph using shoes. Then have each child draw a picture of her shoe to make a pictorial graph of the real-object graph. Compare the real-object graph with the pictorial. Then, if your students are ready, make a symbolic graph of the data. Compare how the same data can be organized in three distinct ways.

Real-object Graph

lace	🥾	👟	👞	👞		
buckle	👞					
velcro	👟	👡				
slip-on	👠					

Pictorial Graph

lace	🥾	👟	👞	👞		
buckle	👞					
velcro	👟	👡				
slip-on	👠					

Symbolic Graph

lace	X	X	X	X		
buckle	X					
velcro	X	X				
slip-on	X					

Assessment Suggestions

Selected Student Outcomes

1. Students develop early understandings of properties of matter, including experience with: liquids, solids, floating, sinking, buoyancy, magnetism, sifting, separating, evaporation, and crystallization.

2. Students develop basic scientific and mathematical skills, such as exploring, predicting, testing, observing, comparing, separating and manipulating materials, sorting and classifying, communicating findings, and analyzing data.

3. Students improve their understanding of the usefulness of graphing as a way to represent data they have gathered and are able to place objects on a real-object graph. Older students gain experience with pictorial and more abstract graphs.

4. Students are able to apply lessons, experiences, and skills gained at all three learning stations to separate materials in a "garbage dump" mixture.

5. Students increase their understanding of how tools and technology are used in science, including magnets, filters, and sifters of varying sizes.

6. Students increase their understanding of recycling and how separation techniques are used in the real world.

Built-In Assessment Activities

For all three learning stations, it is recommended, if time permits, that students be able to explore related and further challenges following the main activity. Several of these challenges are noted below; many others are described in the "Going Further" sections for each activity and could also serve as assessments of student progress.

Learning Station Observations. All of the learning stations in this guide (float/sink, magnets, and sifters) provide excellent opportunities for the teacher to observe student understanding and progress. The teacher can focus on student predictions to see how they change as the activities proceed, and observe how well students understand the challenge and how their learning station behaviors reflect growth in their understanding of science content, as well as development of motor and coordination skills. (Outcomes 1, 2, 5)

Magnet Pre-Assessment. During the introduction to the magnets learning station, the class generates a list of "What We Know About Magnets." This can serve as an indication of their prior understandings. After all students experience the activity, the class again considers the "what we know" list, adding and refining based on what they've now learned. (Outcomes 1, 5)

Separating Garbage. Activity 4, in which students apply what they learned at the three stations to separate a mixture, is a direct assessment of the knowledge and skills students have gained at the three stations. In this sense, the culminating activity of the unit serves as a natural and activity-based assessment for all that has come before in the unit. (Outcomes 1, 2, 4, 5, 6)

Understanding Graphing. The creation of the real-object graph for sinkers and floaters and for magnetic/non-magnetic objects provides an opportunity for the teacher to observe how well students understand the basic idea of the graph. During class discussion about how to interpret the graphs (including the pictorial graph for older students) teachers can assess the ability of students to logically communicate their findings and to generalize from the graph. (Outcomes 2, 3)

Bean Sifting Journal. A "Going Further" for Activity 3 suggests that students write in their journals about the sifters they used and show which bean was separated using which sifter. They could also illustrate their writing. Younger students could draw one or more of the sifters they used. These journals and drawings can help the teacher assess how well students understand the basic principles of sifting, especially the connection between the size of an object and the holes or spaces through which it can fit. (Outcomes 1, 2, 5)

Mixing More "Garbage Dumps." The "Going Further" suggestions for Activity 4 include several possible mixtures as further challenges. One of these, or another of your design, could serve as a direct assessment of students skills and knowledge gained in Activity 4. Students could be asked to explain, either orally or in writing, why they used the techniques they did and comment on their results. (Outcomes 1, 2, 4, 5, 6)

Additional Assessment Ideas

Testing Crayons. Have the class gather a variety of different brands and colors of crayon to see whether they sink or float. Depending on the age of the students, they could investigate and record on a class real-object graph or make a pictorial graph of their own. Older students could write down their ideas about why some float and some do not. (Outcomes 1, 2, 3)

Testing More Materials. Encourage students to test a variety of other objects and materials. Do all soaps float? Do all metals sink? How about all woods? Teacher observation of these explorations and student discussion of the results can reveal student ideas about why objects float or sink, and indicate student growth in applying scientific investigation skills. Teachers could also come up with a list of ten objects and have students predict, on paper, whether or not the objects will (a) float or sink, (b) stick to a magnet, and (c) go through a particular sifter. Their written predictions could be used in assessment. Afterwards they could test all the objects together and make a class chart. (Outcomes 1, 2)

A Pile of Objects. Give students a pile of objects and have them pick a tool to separate the objects into two groups. The teacher can then ask the student why they picked that tool and how the tool helped them. Examples include objects that: stick /don't stick to a magnet; fits into a film canister or doesn't fit; goes through a funnel/can't go through the funnel, etc. (Outcomes 1, 2, 5)

Sifting Through Sifters. Ask students to make a list of all the things they can think of that help people sift or separate materials. Younger students could be asked to draw sketches of the sifters they list, while older students could draw and write brief descriptions. (Outcome 5)

Create-a-Robot. Have students design and draw a robot that can separate the same or similar materials as in the class "garbage dumps." Younger students could explain their robot's functioning orally. Older students should label their drawings and include brief notes on the function of different mechanisms and structures on the robot. You could show older students a colorful drawing of lots of different items and ask them to design a robot that would be able to separate those items. Their design could show how the robot would accomplish this mission. (Outcomes 4, 5, 6)

Literature Connections

Aunt Ippy's Museum of Junk
by Rodney A. Greenblat
HarperCollins, New York. 1991
Grades: Preschool–2

Realizing the importance of reuse, Aunt Ippy never throws anything away. She uses things over and over. Much of her stuff is in her museum—a grand showcase of reuse. The colorful illustrations capture the funny and innovative way Aunt Ippy reuses things.

The Great Trash Bash
by Loreen Leedy
Holiday House, New York. 1991
Grades: Preschool–3

After noticing their town has too much trash and no good way to dispose of it, the animals of Beaston decide to make changes in their everyday life to reduce the amount of trash they make. Full of good ideas, this book is a wonderful extension to Activity 4.

Mickey's Magnet
by Franklyn M. Branley and Eleanor K. Vaughan; illustrated by Crockett Johnson
Thomas Y. Crowell, New York. 1956
Grades: Preschool–2

This is the simple story about the magnet discoveries made by a young boy named Mickey. Although old, it's a classic that may be available in many school or city libraries. Best if read to (or by) the class after they do Activity 2, since it includes some scientific conclusions about magnets that are best introduced <u>after</u> hands-on exploration.

My New Sandbox
by Donna Jakob; illustrated by Julia Gorton
Hyperion Books for Children, New York. 1996
Grades: Preschool–K

A young boy learns that his new sandbox is bigger than he thought, big enough to share with some animal friends and playmates. The boy sees that playing with friends— even when it involves sharing something new and special—is better than playing alone.

Splash!: All About Baths
by Susan Kovacs Buxbaum and Rita Golden Gelman; illustrated by Maryann Cocca-Leffler
Little, Brown, Boston. 1987
Grades: K–4

Before he bathes, Penguin answers his animal friends' many questions about baths, including "Why does the water go up when you get in?" and "Why do some things float and others sink?" Answers to questions are clear and simple. The illustrations opposite the "Why do some soaps float?" page show floaters being turned into sinkers (and vice versa), as students are challenged to do in "Going Further" #1 of Activity 1.

The Tub People

by Pam Conrad; illustrated by Richard Egielski
Harper & Row, New York. 1989
Grades: Preschool–3

Told entirely from their perspective, this is the endearing tale of a family of wooden toys who float and play in a bathtub. The reader becomes emotionally connected to the family, especially when tragedy befalls them. Relief and a sense of well-being come at the end of the book. In addition to connecting to the guide as a "float/sink" book, *The Tub People* could also be considered a "sifting" book given that the child slips through the grating of the drain but the adults don't.

The Wartville Wizard

by Don Madden
Macmillan, New York. 1986
Grades: K–4

A neat and tidy old man earns the title of Wizard when he sends litter back to the people who drop it. Humorous illustrations show the people of Wartville adorned with stick-on trash and wearing bizarre outfits that attempt to hide the trash. This book reminds us that when we're done with something, throwing it away doesn't make it disappear—it must be disposed of properly. The book carries a great message about being responsible for one's own garbage, but does not discuss sorting or recycling.

Who Sank the Boat?

by Pamela Allen
Sandcastle Books/Putnam & Grosset, New York. 1990
Grades: K–2

The reader is invited to guess who causes the boat to sink when five animal friends of varying sizes go for a row. This humorous story—written in rhyme and sporting delightful illustrations—explores the ideas of maximum point (or threshold) and balance. In a "Going Further" for Activity 1 when students are invited to turn a floater into a sinker, threshold and balance could be explored through simple experiments. Teachers who wish to extend the lessons of *Sifting Through Science* to include displacement will be interested in another book by Pamela Allen entitled *Mr. Archimedes' Bath.*

Summary Outlines

Activity 1: Sink or Float?

Getting Ready
1. Decide location of discussion area.
2. Decide location of station and how long it should be set up.
3. Plan a week for free exploration before introducing challenge.
4. Obtain volunteers and copy Activity Task Card.
5. Copy the sink and float signs and glue each to a file folder.
6. Gather items students will test.
7. Make real-object graph.
8. Make pictorial graph (for older students).
9. Set up learning station.
10. Set up introduction area.

Introducing Floaters
1. Hold up object that floats. Ask students to say something true about it.
2. Ask if it will float (thumbs up) or sink (thumbs down). Test object and have students show result with thumbs.
3. What if same object is tried again? Repeat vote, test, and show results with thumbs.
4. Define floater: stays at top of water. Place object near float sign.

Introducing Sinkers
1. Hold up object that sinks and ask for true statements.
2. Ask students to predict with thumbs if it will float or sink. Test object and have students show result with thumbs.
3. Define sinker: stays at bottom of water. Put object near sink sign.

What About Things that Float Partly Underwater?
1. Hold up third object; have students predict. Test the object (it floats partly submerged).
2. Refine definitions: a sinker stays on the bottom; a floater stays off the bottom.

The Learning Station
1. Tell students they'll test things to find out if they float or sink.
2. They'll go to the learning station in small groups.
3. Review the tasks. Send first group to the station.

4. Make sure everyone visits station at least once and freely explores.
5. Explain the discovery nature of activity to volunteers and give them the Activity Task Card.

Introducing the Real-Object Graph
1. Bring real-object graph, objects tested, clear container, and sink/float signs to discussion area.
2. (For older students only) Post pictorial graph; have post-its and pencils/crayons ready.
3. Gather students around real-object graph.
4. Place float and sink signs to head rows of graph.
5. Ask who tested candle, and if it floated. If needed, test again.
6. Put candle in first square of graph in "float" row.
7. Repeat with object that sank, placing it on graph.

Placing Objects on the Graph
1. Hand out one object to every pair of students.
2. Point to object held by a student and ask class to show with thumbs if object floats or sinks.
3. Partner who didn't hold object places it on graph. If a split vote, student re-tests object before placing on graph.
4. After six or seven objects placed, ask, "What do you notice?"
5. Ask, "Are there more floaters or sinkers so far?" Show how to pair object in the "float" row with object in "sink" row.
6. When all objects are placed, ask questions to encourage math, comparison, observation, and communication skills.

Creating a Pictorial Graph (for first and second grade students only)
1. Explain the drawbacks of real-object graph and benefits of pictorial graph.
2. Each pair draws object on post-it. Older students label drawings.
3. Teacher draws candle and object that sinks on post-its.
4. Focus on pictorial graph. Place sink/float post-it labels at head of each row.
5. Ask where to put picture of candle. Put on top square of "float" row. Repeat with picture of sinker.
6. Students raise hands if their picture is a floater, then post on graph. Repeat with sinkers.
7. How is pictorial graph same/different from real-object graph?
8. If possible, leave water table up, and give students further challenges.

Activity 2: Magnets

Getting Ready
1. If possible, set up learning station, without magnets, for exploration a week before magnets activity.
2. Obtain volunteers and copy Activity Task Card.
3. Copy the magnetic and not-magnetic signs and glue each to a file folder.
4. Gather items students will test.
5. Obtain enough magnets for each student to have one. Put eight to twelve magnets at station; keep rest in reserve.
6. Set up learning station.
7. Set up introduction area.

Introducing Magnets
1. Ask, "What do you know about magnets?" Accept all responses; record them.
2. Ask if paper will stick to a magnet. Vote, then test it and show results with thumbs.
3. What about a spoon? Vote, then test and show results.
4. Explain that station has sand with things mixed in it.

The Learning Station
1. Tell students they'll test objects in sand to find out which stick to magnets.
2. Explain that if an object sticks at all to a magnet, that object is considered magnetic. They'll put those objects near the magnetic sign.
3. Ask, "What if an object does not stick to the magnet at all?" [Put it near the not-magnetic sign.]
4. Make sure everyone has time to explore the station.
5. Explain discovery nature of activity to volunteers and give them the Activity Task Card.

Re-Introducing the Real-Object Graph
1. Gather class around real-object graph. Have ready magnet, paper clip, crayon, and magnetic/not-magnetic signs. Place signs at head of each row of graph.
2. Ask who tested a paper clip. Thumbs up if it stuck to a magnet, thumbs down if not. Test the paper clip.
3. Place it on the graph in the row headed by the magnetic sign.
4. Ask about the crayon. Demonstrate it doesn't stick to magnet. Place in first square by not-magnetic sign.

Testing and Graphing More Objects in the Room
1. Each student gets a magnet (or one per pair) to test objects in room.

2. Students must stay with their partners. At your signal, they must stop and listen. Send students off in pairs to explore.

3. Use your signal for attention. Invite pairs of students to choose one small object (magnetic or not) and return with it to discussion area.

4. Have pairs hold up object, invite other students to predict, then place object on graph.

5. If few choose non-magnetic objects, add some to graph.

Discussing the Graph and Generalizing about Magnets

1. Encourage students to interpret graph by asking questions.

2. Point out that scientists/mathematicians use graphs to organize information and understand more.

3. Ask, "What can we tell about things that stick to magnets?"

4. If students say all metal is magnetic, help them modify their statement.

5. Refer to "What We Know About Magnets" list. Should anything be added or changed?

6. If possible, provide further challenges.

7. Remove objects, signs, and magnets; leave sand for Activity 3.

Activity 3: Sifting

Getting Ready

1. Obtain volunteers and copy Activity Task Card.

2. Gather sifters with different-sized holes.

3. Make sure at least some beans can be separated with sifters.

4. Make funnel and container from two-liter bottle. Make paper towel filter.

5. Set up learning station.

6. Set up introduction area.

Introducing Sifting

1. Hold up cup of sand and beans. Ask, "How could we separate the beans from the sand?"

2. Show sifters and ask, "What's the **same** about these three sifters?" "What's different?"

3. Resist temptation to give more instruction. Their challenge is to use sifters to separate beans from sand, and to separate different kinds of beans from each other.

4. Explain importance of careful sifting.

The Learning Station
1. Allow plenty of time for students to freely explore.
2. Explain discovery nature of activity to volunteers and give them the Activity Task Card.

Discussing the Learning Station
1. Gather sifters, bean samples, paper towels, half cup of water, half cup of sand, funnel and filter system.
2. Show class sifter with tiniest holes. Ask, "Was anything able to go through this sifter?" Ask who was able to make a pile of only sand.
3. Choose one type of bean. Ask, "How did you get this kind of bean away from the others?"
4. Repeat with other beans, asking students to explain sifting methods.
5. Did everything go through sifter with the largest holes? What besides sand might go through sifter with tiniest holes?

Separating Sand from Water
1. Pour water into the sand cup. Ask if any of the sifters could be used to separate this mixture.
2. Would sifter with biggest holes work? Try it, and catch what goes through in the empty water cup.
3. What will happen when you pour the mixture through sifter with smallest holes? Demonstrate.
4. Help students draw conclusion that holes in all the sifters allow both sand and water through.

Using a Paper Towel
1. Ask what could separate the sand and water. Give out paper towels and have students hold up to light to see holes.
2. What will happen if mixture is passed through paper towel?
3. Unfold paper towel filter to show it, then refold and set into funnel.
4. Pour sand/water mixture into filter.
5. Review that a sifter with tiny holes is needed to separate something tiny.
6. If possible, have students pursue further challenges.

Activity 4: Garbage Dumps

Getting Ready
1. Make filter systems for each group of four students.
2. Decide how much direction to give students.
3. If possible, arrange for an adult helper.

4. For each student: make cup with salt, sand, pieces of candle, and metal paper clips. Do not stir.
5. Arrange materials for each group of four: four "garbage dumps," four spoons, and two paper cups.
6. Set up other materials for each group: magnets, one half-full water bottle, and a filter system.
7. Line a large tray with black construction paper.

The "Garbage Dump" Activity
1. Ask students if they separate any garbage at home.
2. Explain that scientists and other workers separate garbage without using their hands.
3. Say that the "garbage dump" is made up of pretend garbage.
4. To separate this "garbage," they will apply what they learned at the learning stations.
5. They can move the "garbage" with spoons, but not touch with hands.
6. Pass out "garbage dumps," spoons, and paper cups.

Separating the Wax and Metal
1. Ask what students see in their "dumps." Record. Be sure they know the white particles are salt.
2. Circle WAX on the board. In groups, have students discuss what they learned at sink/float station. Ask, "How can we separate the wax without touching it?"
3. Explain, then have them add water until wax floats, then use spoons to put wax into one of the paper cups.
4. Remove water bottles as students finish pouring.
5. Circle METAL. In groups, have students discuss what they learned at magnet station. Ask, "What tool can we use to separate metal?"
6. Explain, then have students use magnets to move paper clips into the other paper cup. Collect magnets as students finish.
7. Circle SAND. In groups, have students discuss what they learned at sifting station. Ask, "How can we separate the sand from the water?"
8. Explain how they will use the filter system.

Separating the Sand
1. Pass one filter system to each group, and have them begin.
2. Collect cups of wax and paper clips in discussion area.
3. When done, students leave filter system on their table, bring cups of paper clips and wax to discussion area.

What Happened to the Salt?
1. Review how wax, paper clips, and sand were separated. Circle SALT on board and ask, "Where is the salt?"
2. Say you will collect the water they filtered and pour it onto tray with the black paper.
3. Ask what might happen to the water over time.
4. Collect the water, pour it on tray, and set out to dry. Salt crystals should form.

Making the Connection to Recycling
1. Praise class for their skills as "garbage separation scientists." Ask what can be done with the materials they've separated?
2. Ask students who recycle at home how they separate or sort. Discuss questions about the activity or about recycling and the environment.
3. If possible, challenge students with other mixtures. This can also make an excellent assessment.

sink

float

Sink or Float?

Activity Task Card for Volunteers

Your goal is to assist the students in making their own discoveries, while keeping the activity safe, and the mess under control. As needed, remind students of the challenge, but refrain from demonstrating how it is done. Here's what the students are to do:

- Choose an object.
- Predict whether it will sink or float. Tell someone your prediction.
- Test it in the water.
- Place the object on the appropriate sink or float tray.

As students explore, ask open-ended questions, such as:

- What have you discovered?
- What's happening to the object? Is that what you thought would happen?
- Did any of the objects do something different than what you guessed?
- What surprised you?

If students get involved in explorations unrelated to sinking and floating, you might want to steer them gently back on task. Make sure to intervene if you see an unsafe behavior. However, keep in mind that what may appear as "fooling around" can lead to some of the deepest learning experiences. Some of the greatest scientific discoveries have been made when scientists freely and creatively explored and imagined!

Young students need ample time to explore and work with the materials before tackling more structured challenges. Resist the temptation to give explanations to students. Your main role is to keep the station stocked and ready for more students to freely explore it.

Tips for Managing the Station

- If necessary, remind students of the class definitions:

  sinkers: things that stay on the bottom of the water
  floaters: things that stay *off* the bottom of the water (Things that float suspended in the middle of the water should be called floaters.)

- Make sure that everyone tests the **wax candle** and **crayon;** they will need to know that wax floats for a later activity.

- Periodically put objects back on the original tray for more students to test.

- Toss a section of newspaper or towel on the floor to absorb spills if the floor gets too wet.

- Encourage each group to help clean up for the next group.

magnetic

not-magnetic

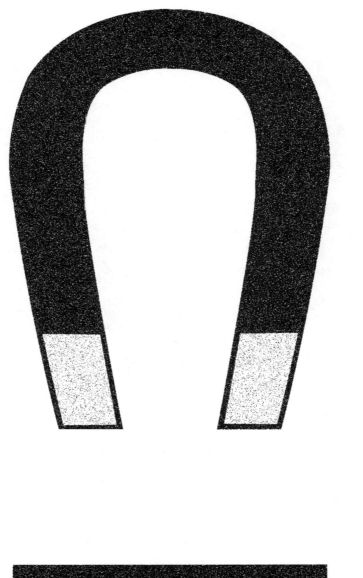

Magnets

Activity Task Card for Volunteers

Your goal is to assist the students in making their own discoveries, while keeping the activity safe, and the mess under control. As needed, remind students of the challenge, but refrain from demonstrating how it is done. Here's what the students are to do:

- Find an object.
- Test it with a magnet.
- Place the object on the appropriate tray.

As students experiment with different objects, encourage them to predict if they will stick to a magnet or not. Ask open-ended questions, such as:

- What have you discovered?
- What's happening to the object? Is that what you thought would happen?
- Did any of the objects do something different than what you guessed?
- What surprised you?

If students get involved in explorations unrelated to the challenge, you might want to steer them gently back on task. Make sure to intervene if you see an unsafe behavior. However, keep in mind that what may appear as "fooling around" can lead to some of the deepest learning experiences. Some of the greatest scientific discoveries have been made when scientists freely and creatively explored and imagined!

Young students need ample time to explore and work with the materials before tackling more structured challenges. Resist the temptation to give explanations to students. Your main role is to keep the station stocked and ready for more students to freely explore it.

Tips for Managing the Station

- If necessary, remind students of the class definition:

  Objects are magnetic if they stick to a magnet at all.

- Periodically put objects back into the sand for more students to test.

- Remind students to try to keep sand in the sand table. Sweep up sand from the floor if necessary.

Sifting Sand and Beans

Activity Task Card for Volunteers

Your goal is to assist the students in making their own discoveries, while keeping the activity safe, and the mess under control. As needed, remind students of the challenge, but refrain from demonstrating how it is done. Here's what the students are to do:

- Encourage students to try all sifters and to explore freely.

- Challenge the students to separate one kind of bean. If a student uses fingers to pick out the beans, say that is one way that works, but suggest that they try to use a sifter to do the same thing.

- If appropriate, encourage students to discover a method for separating each type of bean. They might find they need to sift several times, using sifters with holes of different sizes.

- Ask questions such as, "Which sifter works best for you?" "Why?" "What's your favorite sifter?" "Why?"

As they experiment with different sifters, ask open-ended questions, such as:

- What have you discovered?
- What's happening? Is that what you thought would happen?
- Did any of the sifters do something different than what you guessed?
- What surprised you?

If students get involved in explorations unrelated to separating the beans, you might want to steer them gently back on task. Make sure to intervene if you see an unsafe behavior. However, keep in mind that what may appear as "fooling around" can lead to some of the deepest learning experiences. Some of the greatest scientific discoveries have been made when scientists freely and creatively explored and imagined!

Young students need ample time to explore and work with the materials before tackling more structured challenges. Resist the temptation to give explanations to students. Your main role is to keep the station stocked and ready for more students to freely explore it.

Tips for Managing the Station

- Remind students to sift over the sand tub or one of the trays or box lids.

- Periodically put beans back into the tub for more students to sift.

- Sweep sand off the floor.